The
Sporting Myth
and the
American Experience

The
Sporting Myth
and the
American Experience;

Studies in Contemporary Fiction

Wiley Lee Umphlett

Lewisburg: BUCKNELL UNIVERSITY PRESS
London: ASSOCIATED UNIVERSITY PRESSES

© 1975 by Associated University Presses, Inc.

Associated University Presses, Inc.
Cranbury, New Jersey 08512

PS

374

Associated University Presses
108 New Bond Street
London W1Y OQX, England

A85

U5

Library of Congress Cataloging in Publication Data

Umphlett, Wiley Lee, 1931-
  The sporting myth and the American experience.

  Bibliography: p.
  1. American fiction--20th century--History and criticism. 2. Athletes in literature. I. Title.
PS374.A85U5   813'.083   73-8306
ISBN 0-8387-1363-7

The author thanks Farrar, Straus, & Giroux, Inc. for permission to quote from *American Moderns: From Rebellion to Conformity* by Maxwell Geismar, copyright © 1958 by Maxwell Geismar; from *Fat City* by Leonard Gardner, copyright © 1969 by Leonard Gardner; from *The Natural* by Bernard Malamud, copyright © 1952 by Bernard Malamud; from *Shores of Light* by Edmund Wilson, copyright © 1952 by Edmund Wilson. Reprinted with the permission of Farrar, Straus, & Giroux, Inc.

For Joyce

Contents

Preface   9

Acknowledgments   13

Introduction   17

1 The Background in Classic American Literature   31

2 Encounter with Nature   47
   Introduction   47
   Aleck Maury and the Pursuit of Time   49
   Ike McCaslin and the "Best Game of All"   58
   Santiago: The Meaning of Value in Defeat   69

3 Encounter with Society   87
   Introduction   87
   Jack Keefe and the Code of the Busher   89
   The Neon Wilderness and the Military Machine:
      Two Variations on a Theme   100
   The Message of Satire: The Ex-College Athlete
      and the Groping for Maturity   116

4 The Neo-Romantic Encounter   128
   Introduction   128
   The Death of Innocence: The Paradox of the Dying
      Athlete   130
   The Agony of Rabbit Angstrom: The Search for a
      Secure Self   145
   Roy Hobbs and the Quest for the American Dream   156

5 Epilogue: Some Recent Trends and Variations   169

Selected Bibliography   196

Index   201

Preface

It is a commonplace of American life to relate sports to experience. The minister colors his sermons with athletic metaphors about the "game of life"; business and industrial leaders spice their talks with inspirational allusions to the world of sports; and most Americans poeticize their everyday speech with sports references that have become a part of the language. In fact, sports have become so ingrained in the American experience that we are conditioned to expect and depend on the vehicle of the sporting metaphor to get a point across, emphasize a stance, or underscore a lesson to be learned. After all, sports relate to activity, and Americans have always been obsessed with learning by doing. If sports have conditioned the life-style of the American people, then any attempt to evaluate the relationship of sporting endeavor to the American way of life is integral to understanding Americans as a people. We can perhaps learn more about a people through how they play a game or use their leisure time than we can through how they involve themselves with their day-to-day occupations.

This book attempts to reveal the truth of this observation by recognizing that many of our serious creative writers have been both consciously and subconsciously

9

aware of the significance of sports in American life. In choosing a character of sporting background to write about, the American writer is providing an effective and dramatic method for telling us a great deal about ourselves—our shortcomings, obsessions, and failures as well as our finer moments.

The general plan of this book is based on the study of an archetypal figure familiar to American experience. It does not profess to be the last word on the subject of sports in the genre of American fiction, nor does it attempt to catalogue every writer of fiction who has relied on the sporting experience for subject matter. In fact, as a historical or comprehensive survey the book would run far afield and lose sight of its original objective, which is to reveal to the reader the riches of a special area of American writing and the skill with which selected writers have gone their way in producing serious, influential literature. The study is organized thematically. Selected pieces by representative authors have been chosen for analysis because of their relevance to and illumination of the overall theme as it relates to the development of the archetypal figure of the sporting hero.

The seminal source of this study was an article I wrote some years ago on John Updike's *Rabbit, Run*. It occurred to me then that the central character of that novel persists as the product of diametrically opposed, warring forces in his personal make-up. On the one side, Harry "Rabbit" Angstrom is motivated by an instinctive, inherent desire to identify with the primal simplicities of nature, or a more natural, freer life. On the other side, he is always frustrated in and prevented from pursuing this quest by the restraints and social demands of urbanized society. The result is polarization and the agonizing frustration of an individual, who in attempting to "run" toward a meaningful place in life, ironically stands stock-still.

But the feeling of internal division that enveloped Rabbit Angstrom has descended upon us all during these recent years of doubt and questioning. We see it manifested in various ways, but nearly always expressed in terms of conflict—"dove" vs. "hawk," hippie vs. Establishment, youth vs. age, the have-nots vs. the wealthy, and so on—all these polarities deriving from the one basic conflict between the simple or natural and the complex or societal.

From a special point of view, then, *The Sporting Myth and the American Experience* suggests some of the reasons for the increased polarization of our society in recent years, for in tracing the development of an American literary type from primal innocence to "complex fate," we are, in effect, observing our own moral destiny. How our writers of fiction have used the sporting experience to comment on our moral evolution as a people is what this book is about.

There are certain individuals to whom I am indebted in the preparation of this work: my former advisers and teachers in American literature at the Florida State University, notably J. Russell Reaver and John Simmons, and especially the members of my immediate family for their inspiration and encouragement in helping me realize the "sacredness of achievement."

The University of West Florida
Pensacola, Florida

Acknowledgments

Special permission to quote from certain works referred to in this book has been generously granted as follows:

From *A Radical's America* by Harvey Swados. Copyright 1962 by Harvey Swados. Reprinted by permission of Georges Borchardt, Inc.

From *The American Novel and Its Tradition* by Richard Chase. Copyright 1957 by Richard Chase. From *Ring Lardner A Biography* by Donald Elder. Copyright 1956 by Donald Elder. Reprinted by permission of Doubleday and Co., Inc.

From the book *America's Coming of Age* by Van Wyck Brooks. Published by E. P. Dutton & Co., Inc. and used with their permission.

From *Never Come Morning* by Nelson Algren, Copyright 1942 by Harper and Row, Inc. From "O Youth and Beauty!" in *The Housebreaker of Shady Hill* by John Cheever. Copyright 1958 by Harper and Row, Inc. From *A Fan's Notes* by Frederick Exley. Copyright 1968 by Harper and Row, Inc. All re-

13

Knowles. Copyright © 1959 by John Knowles. From *From Rags to Riches: Horatio Alger, Jr. and the American Dream* by John Tebbel. Copyright © 1963 by John Tebbel. All reprinted with permission of Macmillan Publishing Co., Inc.

From *Hemingway: The Writer's Art of Self-Defense* by Jackson J. Benson. Copyright © 1969 by the University of Minnesota. From *Ring Lardner* by Otto Friedrich. Copyright ̂ 1965 by the University of Minnesota. Reprinted by permission of the University of Minnesota Press.

From *The Landscape of Nightmare: Studies in the Contemporary American Novel* by Jonathan Baumbach. Copyright © 1965 by New York University. Reprinted by permission of New York University Press.

From *Form and Fable in American Fiction* by Daniel G. Hoffman. Copyright 1961 by Daniel G. Hoffman. Reprinted by permission of Oxford University Press.

From *Three Novels of F. Scott Fitzgerald.* Copyright 1953 by Charles Scribner's Sons. From *Aleck Maury, Sportsman* by Caroline Gordon. Copyright 1934 by Charles Scribner's Sons. From "Old Red" in *The Forest of the South* by Caroline Gordon. Copyright 1945 by Caroline Gordon. From "Big Two-Hearted River," "Indian Camp," "Three-Day Blow," "Soldier's Home," and "Fathers and Sons" in *The Short Stories of Ernest Hemingway.* Copyright 1953 by Charles Scribner's Sons. From *Islands in the Stream* by Ernest Hemingway. Copyright 1970 by Charles

Introduction

At one point in *The Huge Season* one of Wright
Morris's characters remarks to another:

> "Old man, a book can have Chicago in it, and not be
> about Chicago. It can have a tennis player in it without
> being about a tennis player."
> I didn't get it. I probably looked it, for he went on,
> "Take this book here, old man—" and held up one of the
> books he had swiped from some library. Along with the
> numbers I could see Hemingway's name on the spine.
> "There's a prizefighter in it, old man, but it's not about a
> prizefighter."
> "Is it about the sun rising?" I said. I knew that was part
> of the title.
> "Goddam if I know what it's about," he said.

American sporting experience, on both an individual
and team basis, has provided the American writer with a
rich source of subject matter, which under the control of
a skilled craftsman can and often does suggest profound
meaning. The work of Ernest Hemingway is obviously a
case in point. It has been observed that throughout the
fiction of Hemingway various games are used as subject
matter, "but more important . . . life itself is often per-
ceived as a kind of game, and many protagonists are
presented as game heroes."[1]

[1]Jackson J. Benson, *Hemingway: The Writer's Art of Self-Defense* (Minneapolis:
University of Minnesota Press, 1969), pp. 73-74.

17

In presenting his heroes' experience through the dominant metaphor of the game or confrontation, Hemingway has forged a vividly dramatic and forceful means of conveying universal ideas about twentieth-century man. From the episodic experiences of Nick Adams to the epic quest of Santiago and even the posthumously published *Islands in the Stream,* the Hemingway vision has dramatized through the ritualistic sports of hunting, fishing, boxing, and bullfighting, modern man's struggle to define himself, not only on a literal but also a deeper, metaphorical level. Similarly, in William Faulkner's "The Bear," the metaphor of the hunt and its attendant mysteries underscore meaning in the story as well as contribute to its profundity. More recently, sensitive and highly talented writers like Bernard Malamud and John Updike have made incisive comments on modern experience by defining anti-heroes with backgrounds in organized sport. Many other serious pieces of contemporary fiction, some highly acclaimed, others less successful, can be singled out as being dependent to some extent upon the sporting scene for meaning and purpose.

Apparently, then, the American writer in his quest to express psychological and moral meaning has recognized that the microcosm of the sporting experience can tell us a great deal about what it means to be an individual in today's world. Accordingly, fictional works with a sporting background seem inspired not only by the fact that "sports are one index to the national genius and character of the American people,"[2] but also by the awareness that

> sport permeates any number of levels of contemporary society, and it touches upon and even deeply influences such

[2]Frederick W. Cozens and Florence S. Stumpf, *Sports in American Life* (Chicago: University of Chicago Press, 1953), p. 6.

disparate elements as status, race relations, business life, automotive design, clothing styles, the concept of the hero, language, and ethical values. For better or worse, it gives form and substance to much in American life.[3]

Richard Chase's work on the American novel has shown how literary expression in America has always tended toward the romance, with our major writers of fiction perennially seeking the proper myth for meaningful expression, a mythological framework that would capture all the contradictions, inconsistencies, and ambiguities of the American experience. Such an intent helps explain why the sporting scene would appeal to the serious American writer. Observe Virginia Woolf's comments on the work of Ring Lardner, a writer who was not taken too seriously until recently:

> It is no coincidence that the best of Mr. Lardner's stories are about games, for one may guess that Mr. Lardner's interest in games has solved one of the most difficult problems of the American writer; it has given him a clue, a centre, a meeting place for the diverse activities of people whom a vast continent isolates, whom no tradition controls.[4]

For a country in which "society" as a compactly organized unit never really existed, the search for identity or a sense of community could be realized through the hunt or the game because these activities demanded for their successful pursuit or performance qualities that Americans have always admired. To a degree, then, participation in sport provides a sense of tradition in itself and a "meeting place" for the author and his reader. It

[3]Robert H. Boyle, *Sport–Mirror of American Life* (Boston: Little, Brown & Co., 1963), p. 4.
[4]Virginia Woolf, *The Moment and Other Essays* (New York: Harcourt, Brace & Co., 1948), p. 102.

is evident, too, that the identification process in sport is psychologically meaningful, because as Reuel Denney observes:

> To play golf, tennis, baseball, or what you will in childhood or maturity engages one in a series of deep and persisting identifications. To play is to belong to some kind of group of more or less definable social and age status.[5]

Yet while meaningful identification through sports may be realized by the reader, in many instances the piece of fiction controlled by what might be termed the "game metaphor," "sportsman's code," or "man-in-motion motif" functions as a means of telling modern man about the illusions he has of himself. Such a purpose is in keeping with the contemporary novel that depends on the ironic mode to express its theme. One might envy the athlete his success in a game but not his failure at meeting the social demands of real life. In *Rabbit, Run* John Updike's ex-basketball player, Rabbit Angstrom, a neo-romantic interpretation of modern man's predicament, is a "man in motion" who seeks something more meaningful than his unsuccessful marriage; yet, for all his "running," Rabbit exists as the example of the "man in motion" who gets nowhere, simply because the world he seeks no longer exists—that world, according to the novel, in which he can again experience the "sacredness of achievement," expressed symbolically in Rabbit's case through the game of basketball.

It is the contention of this study that much serious American fiction, from the pure romance of James Fenimore Cooper to the neo-romanticism of recent years, makes use of figures with a sporting background to give form and meaning to American experience, and that the

[5]Reuel Denney, *The Astonished Muse* (Chicago: University of Chicago Press, 1957), p. 121.

evolution from Natty Bumppo's experience to that of a
Rabbit Angstrom forms the basis for the myth of the
sporting hero in American fiction. However, a query
into the development of the myth raises the big question
of what has happened to the quality of experience between the rendering of a character like Natty Bumppo
and that of a Rabbit Angstrom. In attempting to explore
the ramifications of this question, I shall examine representative examples from American fiction that reveal
the central characteristics of the sporting myth, the concept *myth* for this purpose concurring with that of
Richard Chase: "As it appears in the novel, myth is . . . a
way of sanctioning and giving significance to those crises
of human experience which are cultural as well as
personal. . . ."[6]

In American experience, crisis or tension grows out of
the attempt to reconcile the rift between the dream and
the actuality, in the hope that in doing so the hero may
come to an understanding of self. Here is an experience
that is so indigenous to American fiction that characters
who undergo it often take on mythical dimensions. Since
the search for identity is a major theme in modern literature, this work stresses that the theme's fictional pattern, particularly in regard to the sporting hero, is that
of the *encounter*, implying that the hero of sporting fiction, through his relationship with either nature or society, is confronted with the moral decision of choosing
between a self-effacing code of behavior or his own private self-interests. Like the evaluation of an athlete's
performance, ultimate moral responsibility for the sporting hero depends on the quality of his basic actions.

Here, then, is the psychological basis for the myth of
the sporting hero, whose quest is Jungian in that

---

[6]Richard Chase, *The American Novel and Its Tradition* (Garden City, N.Y.:
Doubleday & Co., 1957), p. 53.

through confrontation he must either face or flee self. Such a conflict—this "essential encounter" that compels the individual to come to terms with self—lies at the center of the American literary tradition. With respect to the sporting myth and American sports, the moral conflict that distinguishes this idea of encounter from other encounters is strikingly expressed in the experience of the sporting hero, since the metaphor of contest or game is an apt symbol or image of the "encounter." In an interesting discourse on Hemingway's method of self-dramatization, Jackson J. Benson justifies the use of the game metaphor in literature:

> the game creates a small, independent world, with its own sharply defined structure of physical consequences, its own laws, its own tribal customs and rituals, its own hierarchy of participants, its own set of conflicts and emotions, and its own set of rewards and punishments.[7]

It is this kind of "world" that defines the quest of the sporting hero in American fiction, a world that expresses itself through organized sport as well as the traditional sports of hunting and fishing.

Implicit in two predominant theories of the origin of organized sport in America is the idea of encounter fomented by the nature-society antithesis. Whether or not one agrees with John Tunis that American sport grew out of the challenge of the frontier,[8] or with Robert H. Boyle that American sport is "urban in impulse,"[9] it is evident that the development of sports in American life owes much to an energetic people's desire to release its energies pent up from facing the facts of existence as they so markedly contrasted with their

[7]Benson, pp. 73-74.
[8]John R. Tunis, *The American Way in Sport* (New York: Duell, Sloan & Pearce, 1958).
[9]Boyle, p. 5.

dreams. It is a basic premise of this work that there is something of both outlooks inherent in the American's desire to express himself through sports, either as participant or spectator. At the same time that the restrictions of city life give rise to the desire to release inner tensions in some sporting endeavor, there is the impulse to return to the primitive but idealized world of nature as symbolized by the sanctified space of the playing area, the heritage of the American's peculiar frontier sense. We shall observe this situation persisting in literature where the hero is confined by city or "system," as Nelson Algren, for instance, projects it through the dissociated experience of Lefty Bicek in *Never Come Morning*.

Moreover, the use of an athletic figure in American literature is enhanced by the fact that in the largest sense of his being he is a figure of innocence, a child existing in the idealized world of "the game," an innocent state further emphasized by his dream of immortality —the desire to remain forever whole and young, or at least for as long as the body can meet the demands of competition. The same dream is even inherent in the life pattern of Natty Bumppo, for, as D. H. Lawrence has noted in his classic pronouncements on American literature, the Leatherstocking Tales "go backwards, from old age to golden youth. That is the true myth of America." In this sense the sanctity or innocent state of the world of the game is symbolically expressed when Douglas Wallop in a contemporary novel has his sports-writer hero remark:

> Sports had meant a great deal to me. A game was a splendid thing, a clean, uncluttered clearing in the confusion of life. A game had precise bounds, precise limits and was played according to precise rules. A game was life in miniature, life idealized. A man and a team were rewarded in direct proportion to their ability and how hard they tried and

how well they cooperated. It was very satisfying.[10]

But the so-called innocent or idealized state of the sporting hero is one of paradox, for through the initiatory rites of "making the team" he confronts experience; yet it is this knowledge that enables him to meet all competition, retain his place on the team, and realize a sense of identity. This polarity of innocence-experience, so essential to an understanding of the American literary tradition, is integral to the sporting hero's function in fiction. Such an antithesis, while more obvious in a work like "The Bear," is more subtly expressed in recent fiction dependent on the ironic mode. Roy Hobbs, the super baseball player of Bernard Malamud's *The Natural*, undergoes a conflict growing out of the disparity between innocence and experience. Ever mindful of his past even while he pursues his dream of the future, he lives in terms of the Edenic innocence of his lost boyhood at the same time that he desires to rewrite the baseball record book. However, the more Roy Hobbs is tested, the greater his inner conflict and isolation from his innocent state, until his ultimate trial of being suspected of throwing a ballgame brings about his tragic downfall.

The hero in American fiction, of course, has always been depicted as individual undergoing trial and as "man in motion." It has been his peculiar heritage to run toward a goal, an experience that would help explain the encounter or initiatory pattern of structure that so much American fiction makes use of. If Updike's spineless hero appears to be running away from any goal, it is only because his experience is the other side of the same coin, an awareness of the need for a goal but a

[10]Douglas Wallop, *So This Is What Happened to Charlie Moe* (New York: W. W. Norton & Co., 1965), p. 135.

hesitancy about how or why one should get there. Updike's circular fictional pattern is indicative of the modern attitude toward existence, where the search for meaningful experience has turned man in upon the mysteries of the self. In an existential sense, then, the very act of "running" or motion itself becomes the meaning for the individual involved, since there is the chance that the act itself will somehow enable him to stumble onto a path to a meaningful goal. Here is the most pervasive and important characteristic of the sporting myth: meaning grows out of the action of the hero himself, or in another sense the significance of the sporting hero's experience is measured in terms of the quality of his performance. The distance between the archetypal Natty Bumppo and his descendent Rabbit Angstrom reflects a similarity in kinds of action, but a change in values.

This change is apparent in the perceptive variations of the athlete as neo-romantic hero in search of self, who, because of the wondrous exploits and achievements of his athletic past, finds it extremely difficult to reconcile the present with the way things were. Although Irwin Shaw's Christian Darling of "The Eighty-Yard Run" is thirty-five years old, he has the immaturity of an undergraduate. In fact, the story is structured in such a way that Darling's return to the scene of what he feels is his life's great moment of achievement—an eighty-yard run in practice—and his actual attempt to re-create the event at the close of the story are end pieces to a series of downhill experiences since that time, serving to emphasize both his lack of maturity and his failure as an adult. Although the hero of the Shaw story possesses the physical traits of the traditional athletic figure, he is almost always a victim of his own emotional deficiency. In a word, Darling's problem is essentially the same as

Rabbit's. Both lack the sensibility necessary to determine the difference between illusion and reality and as a result are incapable of experiencing true feeling or meaningful human relationships.

It is Saul Bellow's contention that the code pursued by the athlete is responsible for much personal confusion in our day, particularly in regard to the meaning of feeling. Joseph, his "dangling man," comments in the opening lines of the novel by that name:

> this is the era of hardboileddom. Today, the code of the athlete, of the tough boy—an American inheritance, I believe, from the English gentleman ... —is stronger than ever. Do you have feelings? There are correct and incorrect ways of indicating them. Do you have an inner life? It is nobody's business but your own. Do you have emotions? Strangle them. To a degree, everyone obeys this code.[11]

Both Darling and Rabbit, as types who lack sincerity and feeling, are incapable of a meaningful love experience. This major theme of modern literature—the failure of love—at least in respect to the sporting hero's experience, is constructed upon his inability to comprehend the alien world of the woman. We will observe this predicament as characteristic throughout the myth, from Natty Bumppo to the contemporary hero, and see that generally the sporting hero fits quite well Leslie Fiedler's observation that in American fiction the typical hero has been coerced into a variety of extra-societal confrontations because of his inherent fear of the sexual encounter with woman, which results in societal ties and responsibilities—the restraints of "civilization."[12]

[11]Saul Bellow, *Dangling Man* (New York: New American Library Signet Books, 1965), p. 7
[12]Leslie Fiedler, *Love and Death in the American Novel* (New York: Stein & Day, 1966), p. 26.

Perhaps the most ironic example of the athlete's code is to be found in James Jones's *From Here to Eternity.* Unlike the hero of Bellow's novel, who feels that regimentation serves to remind individuals of their spiritual brotherhood, Prewitt is a nonconformist in a system —the U.S. Army—whose success is based on the degree of conformity within the system itself. Oddly, Prewitt's ability as a boxer is one of his means of rebelling against the system, for he refuses to become a member of the regimental boxing team. Instead, he persists in being true to his own code in order to enhance his individualism. Still, Prewitt's example of the code exists as merely one more reminder in modern fiction of the intense search for self.

One of the most perceptive works in reaction to the "hard-boiled" code of the athlete because it expresses a sense of personal growth toward the discovery of true feeling is Mark Harris's baseball novel written in the Lardnerian manner, *Bang the Drum Slowly.* Henry Wiggen, ace pitcher for the New York Mammoths, is the first to discover that his roommate, Bruce Pearson, is slowly dying of Hodgkin's disease. As a big-league catcher, Pearson is adequate enough, but his ability to get along with people leaves a lot to be desired, or at least this is what Wiggen, the story's narrator, seems to imply. For a long while Wiggen attempts to keep Pearson's condition a secret, but gradually all the players on the club learn of it. As a result there is a growing respect for Pearson as an individual and for the contribution he makes to a pennant-contending team. The ironic tension that develops between the fact of Pearson as an active player and the knowledge of his impending death helps to reinforce a basic idea of the novel—the worth and dignity of the individual. *Bang the Drum Slowly* is a brilliant combination of the two major traditions of the

American sporting myth. It is at once satirical and romantic in concept, a work whose quality reminds us that indeed serious writing can come out of subject matter that we are often quick to judge as too ephemeral for significant implications.

In summary, then, this study of an archetypal figure contends that American writers use heroes of sporting background to project psychological and moral truths about American experience. Mirroring distinctive American traits, primarily mobility, the sporting hero is an appropriate image of American experience, whose mythical dimensions suggest universal significance. His fictional pattern is the *encounter*, wherein the hero, upon facing the demands of either nature or society, is confronted with a moral decision between a self-effacing code or private interests. This "essential" experience is common to the theme of self-discovery in the whole American literary tradition of the sporting hero. The ensuing sections—Encounter with Nature, Encounter with Society, and the Neo-Romantic Encounter—discuss the satirical and romantic strains of the sporting myth as they manifest themselves in representative works of American fiction.

In the next section we shall see that the sporting hero's experience and its various literary manifestations are tempered by intrinsic characteristics in earlier American literature: puritanical elements, Franklin's "success ethic," the frontier concept, and Emersonian idealism. The interaction of these characteristics contributes to the modern hero's conflict in choosing between a moral code or his own self-interests. The archetype of this figure is James Fenimore Cooper's Natty Bumppo, whose individualistic traits, particularly his self-definition and asocial attitude, derive from his intimate relationship with nature. In such an idealized world Natty, unlike Rabbit Angstrom, exists as the purely romantic conception of the individual confronting the frontier while escaping social demands.

Contributing to the sporting hero's satirical portrait is Washington Irving's Brom Bones who, by protecting his community image from the "outsider," has enhanced the complexity of the contemporary sporting hero. As an innocent type, this kind of character fears whatever seems to threaten his freedom and personal identity. Thus the fear of failure and loss of identity create within him a detestation and mistrust of authority figures and institutions. Because woman represents society's demands and restrictions, he views her as an obstacle to self-realization. The evolution of the traditions begun by Cooper and Irving moves through twentieth-century variations of the encounters with nature and society, culminating in the neo-romantic fiction of recent years. In it we sense that the sporting hero has come full circle, for he reflects a yearning for those essential values that seemed to make the world of Natty Bumppo so meaningful. But the modern hero's encounter experience is complicated by a world that denies him the personal freedom his literary ancestor enjoyed so bountifully.

1

The Background
in Classic American Literature

The myth of the sporting hero in American fiction has its origin in the nature and quality of the American experience itself, the most characteristic feature of it being *mobility*. Even the Puritans, who are most often thought of in terms of their nobility, may be assigned the distinctive trait of mobility, for to them the term connoted not merely adaptability—certainly an important reason for the success of the early colonies—but time put to productive and meaningful use. James I may have sanctioned the setting up of maypoles, among other diversions, as related in his *Book of Sports* (1618), but William Bradford's tone, in reaction to Thomas Morton's "sporting" endeavors, clearly represents the voice of the New England conscience and its feeling about frivolous misuse of time:

> [Morton and his companions] also set up a maypole, drinking and dancing about it many days together, inviting the Indian women for their consorts, dancing and frisking to-

gether like so many fairies, or furies, rather; and worse practices.[1]

Morton and his followers at Merry Mount may be taken as models for the modern country club set, but a "playboy" attitude of self-indulgence could never have helped them overcome the rigors of the frontier, for obviously the new land's demands called for a people as competitive, as willing to accept challenge, and as mobile as the Puritans, or a frontier type who displayed a kind of reckless fortitude toward his terrible new environment. Nevertheless, one senses that the urge to play was in these first Americans, for the demands of mobility create frustrations, and frustrations in turn seek outlets.

As an heir of this prime American trait of mobility, today's athlete, either amateur or professional, has accomplished what appears to be a contradiction. He has turned so-called leisure time into productive time. While at once enjoying or "indulging" himself, he remains symbolic of a kind of life in which one's worth is measured in terms of his degree of success. With the modern athlete, then, mobility is still a virtue, and "the game" has evolved into a kind of last frontier, a projection of symbolic action or the inherent American impulse for self-definition. As a result the modern athletic figure, in his almost godlike status, proves himself highly appropriate as symbol since he combines so many traits Americans revere, traditional characteristics that the heroes of folklore display, which stem from the rugged experience of man against frontier: self-reliance, perseverance, self-assertiveness, competitiveness, practicality, idealism, and an extraordinary physical prowess, marks of not only a durable Puritan but an imaginary Paul Bunyan or

[1]William Bradford, "Of Plymouth Plantation," *Major Writers of America*, ed. Perry Miller (New York: Harcourt, Brace, & World, 1962), 1: 45.

a real-life Daniel Boone as well. What has been rightly observed about the American folk hero can be appropriately applied to the athletic type of hero, also: that he

> appears as a generic expression of the youthful culture which produced him. His characteristic virtues are the qualities of youth: indomitable self-confidence, and a courage in his adaptation to the world which proves almost an heroic denial that tragedy can be possible for *him*.[2]

Witness the professional football player whose exploits are followed by millions on television. As one of the few rugged individualists still among us, he plays with a determination fierce enough to imply that he will never be injured, that he will, in fact, play on indefinitely. That there is something of the folk about the sporting figure, either in real life or fiction, is fitting. His stance as performer of the admirable deed against what sometimes seems impossible odds qualifies him as the perfect modern symbol of American indomitable will. Yet, in contemporary literature the ironic interplay between a man's success in a game and his failure in life contributes a great deal to meaning, effectively illustrating the American writer's preoccupation with the disparity between ideal and fact.

An important attitude contributing to the romantic side of the sporting hero is an obsessive concern for his body, manifesting itself in various cases as a type of sexual narcissism. Such a concern paradoxically stems from the Puritan's outlook on the evils of self-indulgence, and in forming the basis for the code of sport morality has accounted in large part for the internal conflict of the sporting hero in modern fiction. For example, Rabbit Angstrom's worship of self supplants homage to the

²Daniel G. Hoffman, *Form and Fable in American Fiction* (New York: Oxford University Press, 1961), p. 79.

Christian God and crystallizes the central conflict of his story. For Rabbit the sexual act becomes intensely religious in his near-frantic attempt to expand and glorify self. Many athletes, of course, have broken the rules of the training schedule for the lures of the flesh, but these code breakers are usually the first to acknowledge that superior physical performance requires superior physical condition. However, it is his awareness of the puritanical code of self-denial that accounts for the athlete's peculiar selfhood. Somewhat spiritual in conception, it is a self that, because of its frontier sense of superiority in prowess and endurance, is acutely aware of its uniqueness in the romantic sense of apartness, a condition that lends itself very well to expressing the modern theme of alienation. In the Neo-Romantic Encounter we shall see that this "frontier sense" urges a vital but futile return to the essential traits of American experience.

Today it appears that the "success ethic" that originated with the Puritans and found practical application in the life and writings of Benjamin Franklin has been found terribly wanting, and the question is often raised, particularly by our youth, as to why one should seek success in a world of distorted and meaningless values. It is not so ironic that today's youth should be skeptical about success when we consider that a manifesto like *The Greening of America* (1970) looks ahead to a time when the country has returned to those qualities that characterized a youthful, more confident America—those same qualities that define the athletic-hero archetype. Modern fiction has certainly not been lax in criticizing material success and the motives for achieving it, presented usually through the experiences of the aggressive, amoral individual who wins out at the expense of those around him. But in presenting this situation through the symbol of the athlete's past or present experience and relationships—the dramatic rendering of the "success ethic" in microcosm—the writer makes effective use of the ironic mode to either criticize society or to dramatize man's failure to realize his potential. We shall observe these intents functioning in the sections dealing with the encounter with society and the neo-romantic encounter.

The successful businessman, whose ethics in large part derive from the code of the athletic field, is representative of the puritan legacy, which says that success is a sign of God's favor. But increase of wealth means increase of leisure and the resultant problem of equating leisure time with productive effort. Franklin, something of a "sport" himself when he wanted to be, saw no problem, yet revealed his puritan background when espousing his philosophy of sound business sense and the "way to wealth":

> Methinks I hear some of you say, Must a Man afford himself no Leisure?—I will tell thee, my Friend, what poor Richard says, Employ thy Time well if thou meanest to gain Leisure; and since thou art not sure of a Minute, throw not away an Hour. Leisure is Time for doing something useful; this Leisure the diligent Man will obtain, but the lazy Man never; so that, as Poor Richard says, a Life of Leisure and a Life of Laziness are two things.[3]

Like his spiritual father, who effected a compromise between his puritan heritage and the things of this world, the modern businessman has sought to reconcile the world of the sales contract with that of his own leisure time, a situation we find strikingly dramatized in those novels of Sinclair Lewis, John O'Hara, and J. P. Marquand satirizing the country club set. We are especially reminded of the central character in *Babbit* (1922), who appears to be the prototype of the figure who re-

[3]Benjamin Franklin, "The Way to Wealth" in Miller, 1: 121.

lates to sports to enhance his successful image. In such literature it is appropriate that golf is depicted as the significant game of the businessman since the very nature of the game—it has been called "the perfect archetype of American sport"[4]—demands continual self-examination in order to meet the challenges offered on the way to a goal. In a novel like J. F. Powers's *Morte D'Urban* (1962), in which a priest instead of a businessman is hero, the game takes on mythic overtones, but the essential function of the game remains the same: golf is leisure time molded as purposeful action.

The pragmatic philosophy of Franklin joins with the idealism of Ralph Waldo Emerson to permeate the success literature of the last half of the nineteenth century. Despite the difficulty of determining the extent of influence of Emersonian self-reliance on juvenile fiction in the Horatio Alger vein,

> it is possible to estimate that between 1868 and the present there may have been as many as fifty million Americans, possibly more, who read an Alger book. Since they were mostly young Americans in their teens, Alger's influence is inestimable.[5]

In such literature we observe a type of hero whose indomitable self-confidence expressed in terms of effort and accomplishment is really the symbolic representation of Emerson's comments in "Self-Reliance" that

> the power which resides in the self-reliant man is new in nature, and none but he knows what that is which he can do, nor does he know until he has tried. . . .
> a man is to carry himself in the presence of all opposition

[4]Tunis, p. 101.

[5]John Tebbel, *From Rags to Riches: Horatio Alger, Jr. and the American Dream* (New York: The Macmillan Co., 1963), p. 12.

as if everything were titular and ephemeral but he. . . .
And truly it demands something godlike in him who has
cast off the common motives of humanity and has ventured
to trust himself for a taskmaster.[6]

With the development of organized athletics following
the Civil War, particularly baseball and football, the
maxims of Emerson asserting that the inner resourcefulness of the individual should express itself through
action were put to work as part of the coaching
philosophy of these sports. Even the athletic adventures
of Frank Merriwell seemed pervaded with the
Franklinian-Emersonian sense of achieving success. Sub-
standard as literature while attempting to exemplify
their interpretation of the American ideal, the Frank
Merriwell stories enjoyed popularity from around 1896
on toward the 1920s, evolving into the mass-circulated
sports pulps of the 1930s and 40s, but have since passed
into the legend of sports lore. There was no challenge,
either on the playing field or off, that was too great for
Frank to handle, and his exploits on the field are essentially examples of his attitude and policy toward life.
However unreal he may seem, Frank was the per-
sonified ideal in action of what every American boy
thought he could become, simply because the American
way of life led him to believe the mythical accomplishments of a Frank Merriwell possible. If real-life athletes
have not been so versatile as Frank, they have nevertheless emulated many of his feats and thereby set themselves up as heroes to be worshiped and emulated in
turn.
    A better written and therefore more credible kind of
schoolboy fiction was that turned out by Owen Johnson
in the novel *Stover at Yale* (1912), one of the first novels

<hr>

[6]Ralph Waldo Emerson, "Self-Reliance," in Miller, 1: 510-17.

of college life to concentrate on experiences other than those of athletics as part of the college scene. Actually, one of Johnson's main intents in dramatizing his hero's participation in sports is to suggest that playing a game can be serious business. One of the older students advises Dink Stover on his arrival at Yale to "play the game as others are playing it. It's a big game, and it'll follow you all through life."[7] In competition for a varsity position his first year at Yale, Dink senses a conflict that underlies the behavior of many an athlete in a game and in real life:

> For the first time, a little appalled, he felt the weight of the seriousness of the American spirit, which seizes on everything that is competition and transforms it, with the savage fanaticism of its race, for success.[8]

In such writing, too, we find an attitude that has persisted down through John Knowles's *A Separate Peace* (1959). The real enemy is the world of the ivory tower, a world whose impracticality and monastic retreat deny one the opportunity of identifying with the realities of life. Thus the classroom remains vaguely in the background, while the playing field is idealized as an outlet for the expression of individualism. In school or college literature of this kind, then, the playing field or game with its challenges and obstacles approaches the significance of the forest or frontier in our earlier history and literature, while the opponent represents the "outsider" who must be defeated or scourged in order to keep the limits of this world pure and undefiled. We must look back farther into our literary history if we are to comprehend the implications of such an outlook.

[7]Owen Johnson, *Stover at Yale* (New York: Frederick A. Stokes Co., 1912), p. 29.
[8]*Ibid.*, p. 79.

The tradition of the sporting hero in American writing finds its conscious origin in two authors of the Republic who both seemed intent on finding the proper myth to convey American experience. Although both writers used the athletic type of hero to project their understanding of the meaning of American experience, they both relied on contrasting methods to accentuate purpose. Washington Irving's Brom Bones and his triumphant clash with the schoolteacher Ichabod Crane suggest a satirical function, while James Fenimore Cooper's portrayal of Natty Bumppo challenging the wilds of the frontier has a romantic purpose in reminding the American of his uniqueness and potential as an individual. Both writers, however, seem to be aware of what Irving Howe calls "a myth of space . . . a time when men could measure their independence by their distance from each other. . . ."[9] This is an important concept in understanding the meaning of mobility as it relates to the sporting myth.

In "The Legend of Sleepy Hollow" (1820) we witness a time and area in which the distance that separates individuals in a societal sense has begun to narrow, and the existing society, although still somewhat primitive or pastoral, has already begun to impose restrictions on the individual that would limit the expression of personal freedom. One reason for the conflict between Brom and Ichabod is that both antagonists come from distinctively different backgrounds, yet reside within the same community. In other words, the distance between man of action and dreamer has narrowed to the point that the latter is considered an "outsider" and must be banished, even though the social instincts dictate that this act be accomplished through a disguise. In our own day the

[9]Irving Howe, *William Faulkner: A Critical Study* (New York: Vintage Books, 1952), p. 139.

psychic distance between these types has narrowed even further, to the extent that today's athlete in many cases has become a composite of dreamer and doer—a real-life Hank Aaron fictionalized as a Roy Hobbs in *The Natural*. To set records one must have aspirations as well as the physical equipment to accomplish them.

Brom Bones has been identified as "the frontiersman's earliest full-dress appearance in fiction."[10] The same could be said of him as an athletic figure, for like the superior athlete his physical characteristics distinguish him from the other villagers. In "The Legend of Sleepy Hollow" Brom is described as

> a burly, roaring, roistering blade . . . the hero of the country round, which rang with his feats of strength and hardihood. . . . From his Herculean frame and great powers of limb, he had received the nickname of Brom Bones, by which he was universally known. He was famed for great knowledge and skill in horsemanship, being as dexterous on horseback as a Tartar. He was foremost at all races and cockfights; and, with the ascendancy which bodily strength acquires in rustic life, was the umpire in all disputes. . . . He was always ready for either a fight or a frolic.[11]

Because of such physical prowess Brom has an audience of admirers:

> The neighbors looked upon him with a mixture of awe, admiration, and goodwill; and when any madcap prank, or rustic brawl, occurred in the vicinity, always shook their heads, and warranted Brom Bones was at the bottom of it.[12]

Like the modern sports hero, Brom Bones is a figure

[10]Hoffman, p. 58.
[11]Washington Irving, "The Legend of Sleepy Hollow," in *The Sketch Book* (New York: Dodd, Mead & Co., 1954), p. 362.
[12]*Ibid.,* p. 363.

who has status and audience, and his defeat or dismissal of Ichabod Crane, the "outsider," asserts a provincialism akin to the feeling the hometown fans generate toward the local boy who scores the touchdown that beats the visiting team in the later era of organized sports. This provincial attitude or love of place is an integral part of American sport, a frame of mind that inspires detestation of the opponent or "outsider." As a threat to the welfare and prestige of the community, it is imperative that he be defeated.

The fact that Ichabod relates to the women of the story more than to the men enhances his role as opponent of the sporting type. As a singer, dancer, and wit Ichabod can perform those sophisticated things that repel the male rural type. In Irving's words:

> The schoolmaster is generally a man of some importance in the female circle of a rural neighborhood; being considered a kind of idle gentlemanlike personage, of vastly superior taste and accomplishments to the rough country swains.[13]

Actually, Sleepy Hollow as a place where the ". . . population, manners, and customs, remain fixed . . ."[14] approaches the sanctified area of "the game" in significance. Therefore Ichabod can never function as participant in the scheme of things, simply because he does not know the "rules" for participation. In view of his "outsider" role in this early version of the sporting myth, Ichabod Crane stands as one of the first dissociated characters in our literature. A century later Ring Lardner's baseball stories show a similar interest in social structure, since his narrators deceive themselves with the illusion that they are "in" when in reality they are "out." Such self-deception is the basis for the sport-

[13] Irving, p. 355.
[14] *Ibid.*, p. 352.

ing character's encounter with society. Lardner's characters are individuals who know a great deal about the
rules of a game but very little about the rules for successful living. Consider Grimes, the "unlucky" ballplayer
of "Horseshoes" (1914). Like Ichabod, Grimes loses his
girl to another player, whom he terms "the luckiest guy
in the world" since, according to Grimes's point of view,
his rival can do no wrong, either on the field or off.
Unable to gain acceptance into the social structure or
the alien world of woman, Grimes can only present his
side of the story, and in his zeal to show himself in the
right we feel that he may be exaggerating the facts. In a
Lardner story, then, society is the enemy, since it encourages the individual to distort the truth about himself
that he might fit into the order of things; thus, in
Lardner's fiction the testing of a narrator's reliability is
an essential part of the story's meaning, indicative of the
shift in modern fiction to convey meaning through
irony. One wonders how Ichabod would have related his
feelings had the "Legend" been told from his point of
view.

However, the narrator of Irving's story does give us
some important clues to understanding the romantic
side of the sporting myth. He seems impressed by the
idyllic, pastoral-like appearance of Sleepy Hollow, especially after his first youthful adventure in hunting. We
are told: "If ever I should wish for a retreat, whither I
might steal from the world and its distractions, and
dream quietly away the remnant of a troubled life, I
know of none more promising than this little valley."[15]
Compare the sporting experience of Nick Adams in "Big
Two-Hearted River" some one hundred years later,
when Nick retreated to his symbolic stream feeling that
"he had left everything behind, the need for thinking,

[15]*Ibid.*, p. 350.

the need to write, other needs."[16] The paradox of the active man in retreat is a variant of the sporting myth that will express itself at certain other places in this study. In "The Legend of Sleepy Hollow" we observe this antithesis dramatized as a conflict between a dreamer and a man of action, a story that stands as a classic example of functional meaning in fiction and dramatically symbolizes the basic American concern for success through doing.

But it is the romantic tradition begun by James Fenimore Cooper that is the richest in meaning for American experience and the sporting myth. It is richest because, in attempting to measure the worth of the American as individual, it lends itself to broad mythic interpretation in which the wilderness (nature), as opposed to society, is "primal, source and scene of mobility, freedom, innocence. . . ."[17] In the eyes of Cooper's Natty Bumppo, the American is happiest in natural surroundings where, free from civilization's responsibilities, he may pursue a self-reliant existence by confronting the essentials of experience, much as a hunter confronts the day-to-day challenge of providing for himself. With Natty, then, the forest is the great, good place, or inviolable retreat, that which becomes for the modern sportsman the sanctified area of the hunt, the game, or the contest.

But to discover the meaning of the forest's values, Cooper suggests through the experience of Natty that one must abide by the "rules" set up by the natural environment or moral law implicit in it. Natty's attempt to follow these "rules" can be interpreted as the earliest significant reference in American literature to the

[16]Ernest Hemingway, *The Short Stories of Ernest Hemingway* (New York: Charles Scribner's Sons, 1953), p. 210.
[17]Howe, p. 138.

"sportsman's code." This code is purposefully dramatized in chapter 7 of *The Deerslayer* (1841) when Natty (Deerslayer) is confronted with the moral problem of killing his first Indian. Cooper has him think on his advantage:

like
The Bear

> Nothing would have been easier than to spring forward, and decide the affair by a close assault on his unprepared foe: but every feeling of Deerslayer revolted at such a step, although his own life had just been attempted from a cover . . . but instead of advancing to fire, he dropped his rifle to the usual position of a sportsman in readiness to catch his aim.[18]

Natty's code—his courage, initiative, and resourcefulness as well as his sense of honor—all serve to enhance his sporting significance. For Natty, even the superhuman act is not beyond the realm of possibility. Whenever an Indian hurls a tomahawk at Natty, he merely plucks it out of the air and tosses it back at his assailant, usually with deadly accuracy. Frank Merriwell hardly improved on this feat, but the meaning of Natty Bumppo's experience is so closely equated with his deeds that his adventures seem more credible.

Marius Bewley, in defending the credibility of Natty's exploits, has written that *The Deerslayer* is a perfect example in the novel of "action as form," since in this work "the moral and the physical action are intrinsically dependent on each other."[19] In other words, the atmosphere in *The Deerslayer* is one in which the values of its hero are defined and intensified through his actions. Here is an aesthetic theory of fiction that is distinctively modern in outlook. Hemingway was aware of it, and a

[18]James Fenimore Cooper, *The Deerslayer* (New York: The Heritage Press, 1961), p. 98.
[19]Marius Bewley, *The Eccentric Design: Form in the Classic American Novel* (London: Chatto & Windus, 1959), p. 99.

contemporary writer like John Updike has used the theory to significant advantage in *Rabbit, Run* (1960).

Somewhat like the modern athlete, who must perform his deeds within the ritual of the game, Natty abides by the "rules" of his environment to maintain the proper relationship with nature, that way of life which stands for freedom of expression within bounds. Thus Natty senses that he must flee the artificialities of the social order to effect the balance. One critic has expressed the thought that Natty Bumppo is

> the asocial man, free from restraint except for those moral imperatives that bind men in all times and places, who flees the sometimes unjust restraints of a civilized society. . . . But his flight does him no good; it merely begins the cycle anew and makes it all the easier for those social injunctions to catch up with him.[20]

For all his freedom of mobility, Natty chronically worries about what might happen to his ideal world. Similarly, his modern-day counterpart, Rabbit Angstrom, who yearns for the glorious past of his high school basketball exploits, attempts to flee the responsibilities of his marriage, but social demands pursue him and he winds up where he begins. The cycle begins anew, and the motif of running in an ever-widening circle becomes the perfect metaphor of mobility for presenting a large area of twentieth-century experience. Unlike Natty, however, Rabbit seems to sense no "moral imperatives" binding men in all times and places, those imperatives of which Faulkner's Ike McCaslin comes to a fuller awareness after undergoing the ritual of the hunt. The patterns of flight in both Natty's and Rabbit's experience of encounter connote a distinct change in values. In contrast to Rabbit the

[20]Donald Ringe, *James Fenimore Cooper* (New York: Twayne, 1962), p. 36.

ability to distinguish good from evil is the ultimate note of Natty Bumppo's character, and it provides the moral passion of his flight. This flight before the advance of American civilization is virtually a moral judgement on it.[21]

Rabbit's flight, on the other hand, is more than a moral judgment on modern life; it is a judgment on his very character and being. In the neo-romantic encounter the American characteristic of mobility or "frontier sense" is controlled in such a way that it ironically comments on the failures and frustrations of modern experience.

[21]Bewley, p. 111.

2

Encounter with Nature

Introduction

This section, which examines three twentieth-century variations of the tradition begun by Cooper, points out that within the general sphere of the heroes' experience there is a common basis for their action. They all desire to expand the meaning of their lives through close identity with the essentials of nature, even though all three figures come from different backgrounds and react differently within their respective "encounter" experiences.

In *Aleck Maury, Sportsman,* the central figure is an intellectual whose involvement with the world of classical studies has become unreal, so he seeks out a meaning for his existence through the rituals of hunting and fishing. Although he pursues a simple life of noncommitment, Maury's encounter with nature is paradoxically concerned with the larger issues of existence, so much so that he feels compelled to examine his selfhood in the light of the passage of time and the meaning of death.

In growing from boy to man, Ike McCaslin of "The Bear" also matures spiritually as his youthful adventure with Old Ben stays with him and heightens his awareness of the disparity between the way the world is and

47

the way the world should be. Ike's boyhood experience
with nature projects itself into and expands the meaning
of the social encounter of his maturity. Thus Ike is
forced to reevaluate himself in the light of this later experience to arrive at a moral decision.

The most humble and self-abnegating figure of the
three, Santiago of *The Old Man and the Sea,* is paradoxically one of the most positive creations in modern fiction. Disregarding society's values, the old man, through
a self-directed encounter with the forces of nature as
symbolized by a gigantic fish, carves out a code of meaning and honor for himself in such forceful fashion that
even defeat becomes a kind of victory.

Over all three figures hovers the shadow of Natty
Bumppo, who, with his code of fairness, worship of the
primitive, asocial feelings, sense of determination, and
quality of endurance as well as his anti-feminine outlook,
exists as the archetype of the romantic conception of the
sporting hero. Like Natty, all three figures are in pursuit
of a goal which, for all their effort, seems to recede before them. Yet, these characters stand out as the purest
type of the sporting hero in that, through avoiding the
entanglements of society, they have primarily the challenge of nature to face. Nature in this sense is looked
upon not so much as adversary as a necessary environment designed to bring out the best in these figures.
Their encounters, then, bring about a degree of self-
knowledge, and even though their distant goal is never
attained, they come through as better men for having
had their experiences.

It should be noted that characters molded in the
Cooperian manner are so individualized that they express themselves in the main through the traditional and
ritualistic solitary sports of hunting and fishing, certainly
not through urbanized team sports. In fact, as team

members they would lose their significance, because teams exist as communal efforts, their success based on interdependence of performance. With the characters of this section, then, the pursuit, not the goal, is the thing, and accounts in the main for their positive attitudes toward experience.

Aleck Maury and the Pursuit of Time

Time is but the stream I go a-fishing in. I drink at it; but while I drink I see the sandy bottom and detect how shallow it is. Its thin current slides away, but eternity remains. I would drink deeper; fish in the sky, whose bottom is pebbly with stars. I cannot count one. I know not the first letter of the alphabet.

—Thoreau, *Walden*

At one point in "Old Red" (1933), Caroline Gordon's short story of Aleck Maury's old age, the author has her hero reflect on his idea of the meaning of time:

Time, he thought, time! They were always mouthing the word and what did they [his family] know about it? Nothing in God's world! He saw time suddenly, a dull, leaden-colored fabric depending from the old lady's hands, from the hands of all of them, a blanket that they pulled about, now this way, now that, trying to cover up their nakedness. . . . But time was a banner that whipped before him always in the wind. He stood on tiptoe to catch at the bright folds, to strain them to his bosom. They were bright and glittering. But they whipped by so fast and were whipping always ever faster.[1]

The contradiction between society's [his family's] concept of the meaning of time and his own directs the pattern

[1]Caroline Gordon, "Old Red" in *Modern Short Stories,* ed. Arthur Mizener (New York: W. W. Norton & Co., 1962), p. 553.

of encounter in *Aleck Maury, Sportsman* (1934). This novel is a pertinent choice to begin this section dealing with the encounter with nature because Maury's experiences with both nature and society are structured in such a way that they afford us clues not only to Maury's role in the sporting myth but to understanding the social encounters of other major characters in this study.

Educated in the classical tradition, Maury possesses a heightened awareness of the transitoriness of things and events, and his attempt to "catch at the bright folds" and "strain them to his bosom" represents his desire to contain the realities of experience, those things that most people look upon as external facts, merely "a blanket . . . to cover up their nakedness." Thus, Maury's identification with the time-honored rituals of hunting and fishing exemplifies his intense desire to capture the salient moments of life—what, he tells us in the novel, are those "times in a man's life when every moment seems charged with meaning."[2] Maury's impossible pursuit, then, is somehow to find a way to fix reality and make it meaningful.

There is considerable irony in Maury's rejection of the intellectual's life or the contemplative life of the teacher-scholar for the more immediate experience of the hunter and fisherman, for as a professor of the classics he has forged a link with the traditions of the past, but at best the link is artificial and removed from the actualities of immediate experience. In truth, the classical tradition underscores the vanity of human wishes, ironically reminding man of his imperfect condition through knowledge of his greatest achievements. To transcend the human predicament, then, Maury resorts to sporting

[2]Caroline Gordon, *Aleck Maury, Sportsman* (New York: Charles Scribner's Sons, 1934), p. 88.

ritual, for he is sensitively aware that the significance of the ritual act lies in its ordering power and sense of the past's continuity. If one is to contain the passage of time, he must directly identify through ritual with that which is timeless; so in Miss Gordon's novel her protagonist's life is presented as a perennial quest for forest and stream. Even in his old age, when he is compelled to give up the rigors of the hunt for fishing, Maury reasons:

> "a man can fish as long as he lives. . . . Why, one place I stayed last summer there was an old man ninety years old had himself carried down to the river every morning. . . . Yes, sir, a man can fish as long as he can get down to the water's edge."[3]

It is the imagery of fishing that predominates in *Aleck Maury, Sportsman,* and its function is akin to Thoreau's use of it in his tract on the meaning of man and nature, *Walden* (1854). To recover the verities of "eternity" is not an intellectual process for Thoreau ("I know not the first letter of the alphabet," he tells us); rather, this quest consists of an intuitive recognition of the realities that underlie external facts. Hence his metaphor of time as a stream and himself as a fisherman. In a metaphorical sense, man enhances his being and meaning through plumbing the stream of history or time as it is revealed through nature. The timeless ritual of hunting and fishing, then, is one way of perpetuating self, and Maury's rejection of the ivory tower for the more immediate experience of gun and rod reflects the American's basic suspicion of academia (the Ichabod Crane type), while pointing out a process that has been termed "the typical self-discovery of the American character which has been

[3]Gordon, "Old Red," p. 563.

conceived as an immersion in experience, rather than a contemplative withdrawal."[4]

Such a life of contemplation he had escaped, Maury tells us in "Old Red": "A few translations from Heine in his courting days, a few fragments from the Greek, but no, he had kept clear of that on the whole. . . ."[5] In the novel Maury's "escape" or flight, which parallels that of his great antecedent, Natty Bumppo, is externalized by his repeated efforts to locate the perfect spot for fishing. In the meantime the impracticality of his classical education, which prepared him primarily for teaching Latin and Greek, is emphasized throughout. After a series of odd jobs at various places in the country, Maury takes on the first of his academic positions, that of a rural schoolmaster in Tennessee. The ensuing years find him accepting new appointments throughout the South, but always with the primary end in mind of finding better fishing. The novel ends with Maury, an old man, returning to a favorite spot in Tennessee to fish out his remaining days.

Despite the apparently simple narrative of this book, Maury's quest is fraught with profound implications, and in a sense his kind of mobility *is* a kind of "contemplative withdrawal," much like that of Thoreau's. But in another, more positive sense, Maury's flight is similar to Thoreau's in that it represents a setting forth toward a goal, an attempt to "live deliberately, to front only the essential facts of life" by paradoxically turning away from the restraints of society and yielding to the experience of nature, thereby encountering one's true self as a Natty Bumppo would. An example to Maury of the failure to "live deliberately" is his intellectual son-in-law, Steve, who seems "dead to the world." Yet he makes

[4]Hoffman, p. 80.
[5]Gordon, "Old Red," p. 553.

Maury ironically realize that "it was he, not Steve, that was the queer one! The world was full of people like this boy, all of them walking around with their heads so full of this and that they hardly knew where they were going."[6] Thus Maury has a self-awareness and a sense of mobility that the other characters of Miss Gordon's world lack. To him, to know where one is going can best be realized when life is lived at its simplest, divorced from books and their persistent reminding of the complexities of civilization, unencumbered even by the restrictions of married life. As Maury himself reminds us in the novel, to a sportsman "no really good day is ever long enough. People as a rule do not understand this. They think that a man goes fishing to kill time. They do not realize that every day of good sport is one of unremitting, exhausting effort."[7]

In this respect Maury's southern background must be considered as an important factor contributing to his concern for the physical realities of experience and his fascination with the simple. He shows a great admiration for Negroes for much the same reason that Natty Bumppo admires Indians. Understanding the primitive ways of a primitive people equips one to get closer to the secrets of nature. "It's wonderful how much you can learn from niggers," Maury remarks at one point in "Old Red," referring to the old black woman who has taught him "how to smell out" fish.[8] The old woman's special talent is an intuitive process that underscores how man should approach the mysteries of nature. It is a process, too, that most people of civilized or societal background can never comprehend. Even the humble dwelling places of the southern rural Negro become

[6]*Ibid.*, p. 562.
[7]Gordon, *Aleck Maury*, p. 98.
[8]Gordon, "Old Red," p. 554.

idealized in Maury's mind, simply because they are close to the essentials he is seeking:

> The field slanted straight down before him to where the pond lay, silver in the morning sun. A Negro cabin was perched halfway up the opposite slope. A woman was hanging out washing on a line stretched between two trees. From the open doorway little Negroes spilled down the path toward the pond. Mister Maury surveyed the scene, spoke aloud:
> "Ain't it funny now? Niggers always live in the good places."[9]

Thus, Maury's respect for things simple, his resistance to change, his ability to see objects and creatures as real in themselves and yet as mysteries, reflect not only his southern heritage but the primary fact that his relationship with nature is religious in intensity. It is Maury's ritualistic performance of sportsman as priest that enables him to realize order and stability in a changing society that is the new South.

Paradoxically, though, it is the clash between Maury's religious sense of nature and his intellectual awareness of the imperfections of the human condition as symbolized by the passage of time that creates a crisis in his mind that can never be resolved. The novel's title identifying Maury as "Sportsman" has a somewhat ironic function, for Aleck Maury *is* a scholar, and this very fact denies him an integral part in the natural scheme of things, since the true sporting role demands impulsive, intuitive response. No matter how hard he may try, Maury can never really divorce himself from the objective facts of existence as he knows they are. Once aware of the philosophical implications of history and art as revealed through study of the classics, one can never effect a "return to nature" in the true sense of the phrase.

[9]*Ibid.*, p. 559.

The cycles of civilization all ended in decay; only nature has persisted, but a self-awareness of this difference, like Maury's, gives one a heightened perception of impending death and the mutability of things, not only in a social sense but in an individual one as well.

In light of the internal conflict growing out of his essential encounter, then, "Aleck Maury's vision of life is never very far from the terror of death."[10] Hence his continual search for the perfect fishing spot symbolizes his futile attempt to perpetuate himself. Also, Maury's search represents his symbolic fortress against his subconscious adversary, death itself. But as nature represents the continuing life cycle, so death is essential to its renewal, and in Thoreau's retreat we see this fact symbolized not only in regard to the seasons but to the spirit of man as well. In contrast to the codes set up for their heroes by Cooper, Faulkner, and Hemingway, the code of Aleck Maury expresses itself as a form of flight from the inevitable. Unlike Natty and even Thoreau, Maury can never wholly become the natural man immersing himself in the basic realities of the woods around him. Natty, in fleeing the restrictions set up by society, has no family ties or formal learning to speak of. Directly involved with the ritualistic patterns of nature, with no barrier between himself and the experience, Natty is never bothered by the fear of death because he sees it as a part of the natural order of things, a realization that occurs to him many times, especially at one point in *The Deerslayer* when he arrives at Lake Glimmerglass, another symbol of the sportsman's retreat:

> "This is grand!—'tis solemn!—'tis an edication of itself, to look upon!" exclaimed Deerslayer, as he stood leaning on his rifle . . . "not a tree disturbed even by redskin hand, as I

[10]Frederick J. Hoffman, "Caroline Gordon: The Special Yield," *Critique* 1 (Winter 1956): 35.

can discover, but evrything left in the ordering of the Lord, to live and die according to his own designs and laws!"[11]

Thus, by the end of *The Prairie* (1827), Natty, as an old man, willingly accepts the advent of death.

On the other hand, the demise of immediate members of Maury's family serves to reinforce his attitude toward death and the central encounter of his existence. Significantly, his son Dick is drowned in one of Maury's idyllic streams, a tragedy that helps build a wall between Maury and his wife, Molly, until their relationship culminates in the greatest estrangement of all, her death. But even freedom from the demands of family life cannot curtail Maury's frantic flight before the idea of death, and his predicament is even more emphatically delineated when, like Old Red the fox, with whom he can be equated, Maury becomes more the hunted than the hunter. Toward the end of the novel he tells us what it was he had always feared: ". . . that this elation, this delight by which I lived might go from me. . . ."[12] In "Old Red" the past keeps impinging upon the present until finally in Maury's mind the past becomes identified with the old fox itself, elusive and defying capture. Yet in another sense, Maury's identification with Old Red serves as a reminder that he is not only a victim of the past but imprisoned by it as well.

Wright Morris in *The Huge Season* (1954), a novel that deals with a similar problem, depicts his main character, Peter Foley, also an intellectual, as overcoming the tyranny of the past by relating his memories to the immediate necessities of the present. In the fiction of Morris where the real enemy is nostalgia, the past becomes useful insofar as it enables his characters to achieve

[11]Cooper, p. 21.
[12]Gordon, *Aleck Maury*, p. 224.

self-knowledge. The sporting figure, Charles Lawrence, who as a great tennis player exists in Foley's mind as a symbol of the 1920s, has a function similar to that of Old Red's in the mind of Aleck Maury. But whereas Foley's memories of Lawrence help him to disengage the past from the present and thereby gain a truer picture of his present existence, Maury's memories of Old Red only serve to show him as irrevocably involved in the past.

Like that of most Southerners, Aleck Maury's life is controlled by a pattern of existence designed to establish order and meaning. But his attempt to recapture the past through identification with nature is merely superficial. Like the pattern of life in classic civilization, on which he is an authority, a way of life has been imposed on the natural. In other words, Maury has essayed to forge a classic piece of art out of his life by devising a code that stresses the stability and continuity of things. His outlook, in spite of its individualistic approach to life, is one that is controlled by the dictates of tradition. At best it is merely artificial, for by the close of the novel Maury is still searching. In the encounter of Aleck Maury, pursuit can be equated with flight. Wright Morris's observation, then, holds true for Aleck Maury as sporting hero: "*Flight* always cuts two ways: it is both toward something and away from something."[13] Even though Maury's peculiar kind of mobility—his perennial quest for forest and stream—is a search that in its religious intensity reflects kinship with other variations of the sporting hero confronting the demands of nature, his increased awareness of man's imperfections undermines the basically innocent nature of the romantic type of sporting hero.

[13]Wright Morris, *The Territory Ahead* (New York: Atheneum, 1963), pp. 69-70.

Ike McCaslin and the "Best Game of All"

> "It's the gun," Sam said. He stood beside the fence, motion-
> less, the old man, son of a Negro slave and a Chickasaw
> chief. . . . *The gun,* the boy thought. *The gun.* "You will have
> to choose," Sam said.
>
> —Faulkner, "The Bear"

In contrast to the self-indulgent, nostalgic outlook of
Aleck Maury, Ike McCaslin of William Faulkner's "The
Bear" (1942) has a disenchanted view of his southern
past. He realizes it not as a time filled with the idealized
achievements of his ancestors but as one that has been
tainted with the evils of land profiteering, slavery, and
miscegenation. Accordingly, the encounter pattern, in
expressing itself through Ike's experience—from his
youth to the renunciation of his heritage—is based on
"his effort to reconcile wilderness and society, or failing
that, to decide which will allow and which frustrate the
growth of moral responsibility."[14] But because of his
youthful adventures in the ritual of the hunt, Ike's "essential encounter" gives him a perceptive understanding
of his natural relationship to the wilderness. Long before he was sixteen he had heard "the best of all talk-
ing":

> It was of the wilderness, the big woods, bigger and older
> than any recorded document. . . . It was of the men, not
> white nor black nor red but men, hunters, with the will and
> hardihood to endure and the humility and skill to survive,
> and the dogs and the bear and deer juxtaposed and re-
> liefed against it, ordered and compelled by and within the
> wilderness in the ancient and unremitting rules which void-
> ed all regrets and brooked no quarter;—the best game of
> all.[15]

[14]Howe, p. 92.
[15]William Faulkner, "The Bear" from *Go Down, Moses* (New York: Modern
Library, 1942), pp. 191-92.

To Ike, hunting is the "best game of all" because its "rules" properly relate the individual not only to the wilderness or one's natural environment but also to his fellowman. Consequently, the sporting encounter becomes a kind of moral education for Ike, suggestive of much more than a "ritual-game in which the virtues of restraint, honor, and comradeship are embodied,"[16] or a "duel enacted within a solid set of conventions and rules, faultlessly observed by both sides."[17] Ike's encounter is an experience in self-discovery that enables him to transcend the illusion of the past and to examine himself in the light of what really happened, thus compelling him to look squarely at the issues and make a moral decision. The decision Ike McCaslin makes places him along side Hemingway's Santiago as among the most forceful sporting figures in modern fiction.

The metaphorical implications of the hunt are necessary to the meaning of "The Bear," because this "best game of all" demands of its participants that they be "ordered and compelled by and within the wilderness." As any performer in a game of modern organized sport must abide by the rules to maintain order within the sphere of the game or else risk penalty or banishment, so must the ritual of the hunt be carried out within the realm of the wilderness according to its laws. Thus, hunting rites and their execution imply adherence to a moral code, the infraction of which can bring down disaster upon the "rules breaker." By extension and through Ike's growing awareness of the moral nature of the hunt, the evils of the southern past are expressed as being outside the natural order and therefore condemned.

[16]Howe, p. 255.
[17]R. W. B. Lewis, "The Hero in the New World: William Faulkner's 'The Bear' " in *Bear, Man, and God,* ed. Utley, Bloom, and Kinney (New York: Random House, 1964), pp. 308-9.

As in Caroline Gordon's fiction discussed in the preceding section, the concept of pursuit is integral to understanding the central meaning of "The Bear." Faulkner himself has answered queries about this work, that

> the hunt was simply a symbol of pursuit. Most of anyone's life is a pursuit of something. That is, the only alternative to life is immobility, which is death. This was a symbolization of the pursuit which is a normal part of anyone's life, while he stays alive, told in terms which were familiar to me and dramatic to me. . . . Always it's the greater part of pleasure, not to destroy what you have pursued. The pursuit is the thing, not the reward, not the gain.[18]

Whereas Aleck Maury's fear of "immobility" drives him to a frantic pursuit for a way of perpetuating self, Ike McCaslin's pursuit of an unattainable ideal compels him to reevaluate self in the light of a new understanding of his legacy. With the slaying of Old Ben, symbol of the untainted natural life of the wilderness, Faulkner makes use of the perfect objective correlative to project the significance of Ike's growing awareness of his relationship to both past and present. Each confrontation of Old Ben during Ike's youth becomes another crucial step toward his "essential encounter," culminating as it does with the renunication of his heritage at the age of twenty-one for a simpler life unencumbered by the evils of a social order.

Another point to remember when analyzing the pursuit element and its relationship to Faulkner's overall intent in this story is revealed in Warren Beck's observation that ". . . Faulkner's conceptual power . . . renders the vision of life as motion . . . reverberant of past experience and projective of attitudes and action."[19] In fact, Faulk-

[18]Frederick L. Gwynn and Joseph L. Blotner, eds., *Faulkner in the University* (Charlottesville: University Press of Virginia, 1959), pp. 271-72.

[19]Warren Beck, *Man in Motion: Faulkner's Trilogy* (Madison: University of Wisconsin Press, 1961), p. 8.

ner himself has declared that "Life is motion" and that "The aim of every artist is to arrest motion. . . ."[20] What Aleck Maury attempted to accomplish in his fictionalized life, Faulkner essayed to achieve in his writing, and this athletic-like theory of writing has inspired some provocative studies on the nature of Faulkner's fiction.[21] Thus, in "The Bear" we observe Ike McCaslin represented in the tradition of the sporting hero as an individual in motion, whose action reflects his attitude toward life. From his early youth on, Ike exists as one compelled to pursue and seek out an inner destiny, that destiny Faulkner dramatizes so challengingly in Part IV of the story when Ike examines the evidence of his legacy as revealed in the ledgers of his grandfather.

Actually, Ike admits, his encounter pattern had begun long before he was ten years old, when he had first been brought to camp "to earn for himself from the wilderness the name and state of hunter provided he in his turn were humble and enduring enough" (p. 192). In fact, it had really all begun—all that Old Ben, "the shaggy tremendous shape," stood for—in the collective unconscious of Ike's dreams. Or as Faulkner expresses it, the meaning of Old Ben

> ran in his knowledge before he ever saw it. It loomed and towered in his dreams before he even saw the unaxed woods where it left its crooked print, shaggy, tremendous, red-eyed, not malevolent but just big, too big for the dogs which tried to bay it, for the horses which tried to ride it down, for the men and the bullets they fired into it; too big for the very country which was its constricting scope. It was as if the boy had already divined what his senses and intellect had not encompassed yet: that doomed wilderness

[20]See Jean Stein's *Paris Review* interview of 1954.

[21]Two works worthy of mention here are Walter J. Slatoff's *Quest for Failure: A Study of William Faulkner* (Ithaca, N.Y.; Cornell University Press, 1960) and Richard P. Adams's *Faulkner: Myth and Motion* (Princeton, N.J.: Princeton University Press, 1968).

> whose edges were being constantly and punily gnawed at by
> men with plows and axes who feared it because it was
> wilderness . . . where the old bear had earned a name, and
> through which ran not even a mortal beast but an anach-
> ronism indomitable and invincible out of an old dead
> time. (p. 193)

Old Ben, of course, is equated with the wilderness and
what it stands for, and his mythical stature is of such
proportion and pith in the mind of the young Ike that
each ensuing November brings with it the realization
that the men he knows so well are going to the big
woods "not to hunt bear and deer but to keep yearly ren-
dezvous with the bear which they did not even intend
to kill. Two weeks later they would return, with no
trophy, no skin" (p. 194).

The paradox of the hunt with "no trophy, no skin"
suggests preference for the pursuit or the continuation
of an idealized community (the hunting camp) as opposed to the false standards of a man-made society.
Thus when Ike expresses that "it seemed to him that at
the age of ten he was witnessing his own birth," he is
subconsciously asserting his belief that his association
with the hunt will help teach him those redeeming values that have been warped by the social order. From this
point we witness each confrontation of Old Ben prepar-
ing Ike for the inevitable choice he must make. After
coming across the bear the first time with Sam Fathers,
Ike realizes later that "he knew what he had heard in
the hounds' voices in the woods that morning. . . . It was
in him too . . . a sense of his own fragility and impotence
against the timeless woods, yet without doubt or dread"
(p. 200). The first stage in Ike's quest for self-knowledge
is realization of his own mortality through contact with
the wilderness in the mature manner of Natty Bumppo,
not Aleck Maury. The desire for immortality is a perva-

sive characteristic of the sporting hero, but only the more mature character grows to realize that he can gain his life by losing it. Next, Faulkner emphasizes Ike's moral growth by having him express a desire to look upon Old Ben. But the next year when he has his own gun for the first time, Ike is reminded by Sam that "You ain't looked right yet." Sam implies that Ike must make a choice and another step toward maturity.

To look upon nature, Sam suggests, one must do so from the proper perspective: abide by the rules nature has drawn up and reject those deceptions and inventions that society has devised to give it the advantage. Thus Faulkner tells us that Ike in relinquishing his gun "had accepted . . . a condition in which not only the bear's heretofore inviolable anonymity but all the ancient rules and balances of hunter and hunted had been abrogated" (p. 207). But even this condition is not enough. "He was still tainted" by holding onto his watch and compass, and Ike realizes that he must rid himself of even them. In the picture Faulkner draws at this point we sense something of the primitive innocence that is a necessary part of the makeup of the sporting hero: "He stood for a moment—a child, alien and lost in the green and soaring gloom of the markless wilderness. Then he relinquished completely to it" (p. 208). Like the sporting figure of modern organized sport who must make a personal sacrifice to perform proficiently within the code of his chosen sport, Ike McCaslin now stands ready to perform and receive what the wilderness has to offer him. As a result, he sees the bear:

> It did not emerge, appear: it was just there, immobile, fixed in the green and windless noon's hot dappling, not as big as he had dreamed it but as big as he had expected, bigger, dimensionless against the dappled obscurity, looking at him. Then it moved. It crossed the glade without haste,

walking for an instant into the sun's full glare and out of it, and stopped again and looked back at him across one shoulder. Then it was gone. It didn't walk into the woods. It faded, sank back into the wilderness without motion as he watched a fish, a huge old bass, sink back into the dark depths of its pool and vanish without even any movement of its fins. (p. 209)

The imagery of the bear, woods, and fish is a vivid choice in conveying to the reader the sense of Ike's identifying with something that is so elemental in nature that it merges wholly with it. As another characteristic of the sporting myth, this feeling of oneness within the sphere of sporting endeavor helps Ike to comprehend his part in the whole and take yet another important step toward moral responsibility.

"So he should have hated and feared Lion," Part II begins, suggesting that Ike recognizes in Lion, the mongrel dog of fierce determination, a sure means of tracking down Old Ben, thereby threatening the way of life the big bear represents. Yet, Faulkner relates, Ike did not hate and fear Lion. Instead

it seemed to him that there was a fatality in it. It seemed to him that something, he didn't know what, was beginning; had already begun. It was like the last act on a set stage. It was the beginning of the end of something, he didn't know what except that he would not grieve. He would be humble and proud that he had been found worthy to be a part of it too or even just to see it too. (p. 226)

With Lion as a part of the pursuit, the search for Old Ben comes to an end as does Ike's education in the ways of the wilderness, which all began, as Faulkner tells us, with Sam Fathers as Ike's mentor; the wilderness, his college; and Old Ben himself, his alma mater. In this "educational" program Lion's courage symbolizes the necessary requirement Ike must possess to face his crucial test or encounter.

Before the advent of Lion, Ike, like the other hunters, is powerless before the presence of Old Ben, as when he confronts the bear for the second time:

> it seemed to the boy that it would never stop rising, taller and taller . . . it seemed to him that he was directly under the bear. He could smell it, strong and hot and rank. Sprawling, he looked up where it loomed and towered over him like a thunderclap. It was quite familiar, until he remembered: this was the way he had used to dream about it.
> Then it was gone. (pp. 211-12)

At this point in the story we sense that Ike has not been taught the proper lesson in courage, a lesson he will learn from his admiration of Lion's role in the pursuit, which "showed him that, by possessing one thing other, he would possess them both" (p. 296); that is, by showing courage he would learn humility and pride, those essential characteristics of the true sportsman. With Lion, then, who also stands for the quality of endurance, the pursuit begins to take a fatal turn for Old Ben, and Ike is now closer to being prepared for his encounter with society.

When Boon Hogganbeck and Ike take off for Memphis at the beginning of Part III to replenish the camp's liquor stock, Faulkner weaves in the anti-urban attitude that appears in most literature drawing upon the sporting scene for subject matter. Whereas life had been simple and meaningful in the camp,

> in Memphis it was not all right. It was as if the high buildings and the hard pavements, the fine carriages and the horse cars and the men in starched collars and neckties made their boots and khaki look a little rougher and a little muddier and made Boon's beard look worse and more un-

shaven and his face look more and more like he should never have brought it out of the woods at all. (p. 231)

Plainly here and in the ensuing parts of the Memphis episode Faulkner insists that these two sojourners are out of their natural element, particularly Ike, who must now contend with a drunken Boon, a situation that in itself comments on the social order. But back at camp Ike again becomes central when the hunt is set and General Compson chooses him to ride the hunt mule.

The scene is ready, then, for that "last act on a set stage," the significance of which Ike will carry with him throughout the rest of his life—the slaying of Old Ben, the deaths of Lion and Sam Fathers, events that close out Ike's "education" and enhance the meaning of his imminent encounter with the order outside the wilderness. All three events, as a part of his initiatory rites, have taught Ike the qualities necessary for him to make his moral choice:

> an old man, son of a Negro slave and an Indian king, inheritor on the one hand of the long chronicle of people who had learned humility through suffering . . . led him as though by the hand to where an old bear and a little mongrel dog showed him that, by possessing one thing other, he would possess them both. (pp. 295-96)

Here again is shown that the sporting myth is involved with primitive virtues, this time ingeniously and ironically symbolized in an individual of mixed background, which, as a composite of the most persecuted groups in American history, dramatically illustrates the heroic possibilities of endurance and suffering.

In Part IV, when Ike is twenty-one and ready to come into his inheritance, his past forms a prominent backdrop against which his immediate predicament is made to stand out sharply. The parallel is a necessary one, for the lesson Ike has learned in the wilderness has made him at the age of twenty-one critically aware of the great distance between the noble actions of men governed by nature and the petty ones of men restricted by the laws of society. Just as he, ten years before, had realized in giving up the devices of man that he could learn more readily what nature had to offer him, so he now feels that he must "relinquish" his material heritage, the land bequeathed him by his grandfather, if he is to comprehend what it really means to be "free." The ledgers of Carothers McCaslin, in which were kept the records of his land and slave holdings, serve to remind Ike that the land was never really anybody's to bequeath. Rather, man was created ". . . to hold the earth mutual and intact in the communal anonymity of brotherhood, and all the fee the Creator asked was pity and humility and sufferance and the sweat of his face for bread" (p. 257). In the sporting myth the sphere of activity, whether it be contained by the boundaries of the wilderness or the game, is set for all participants alike. The "rules" see to that end. Ike's having abided by the rules of the wilderness has taught him a lesson that has inured him for his essential encounter.

Because of those who have broken the rules, Ike recognizes that the land has been cursed but that he can redeem himself by Christlike renouncing and enduring the existing order according to the right rules, such self-denial becoming in itself a kind of freedom. Like his sporting brothers, Ike again recognizes primitive virtues by citing the Negro as exemplifying endurance since, because of his plight, the Negro is "better" and "stronger" than the white man; thus from an ironic point of view the story reflects an "enlarging compassion for the defeated."[22] This theme is also treated in depth

[22]Howe, p. 153.

by Ernest Hemingway, who, in creating a sporting hero engaged against nature while simultaneously involved with nature, asserts that the individual can effect victory out of apparent defeat by pursuing a personal code of self-realization.

In the world of Ike McCaslin there is no place for the feminine attitude, that outlook which seeks to remind men of their social obligations, yet another example of a sporting-myth characteristic harking back to Natty Bumppo. It is the woman who denies the sporting hero his self-definition and sense of personal freedom by coercing him into unnatural patterns of behavior. For Ike the idealized world of the hunting camp had been a womanless existence. Later, after his marriage, he is made even more aware of his personal commitment to that world when his wife urges him to accept his inheritance. In assessing his wife's demands Ike indicts all women, particularly for their sexual roles:

> She already knows more than I with all the man-listening in camps where there was nothing to read ever even heard of. They are born already bored with what a boy approaches only at fourteen and fifteen with blundering and aghast trembling.[23]

His wife's voice is that of social demands tempting the innocent yet real world of essential values. But Ike resists to the end, and his pattern of behavior in this story is designed to retain his innocence, because the world of the hunt has reminded him that "still the woods would be his mistress and his wife" (p. 326).

The final section of "The Bear" exists as a commentary or pastoral lament concerning the passing of not only the wilderness but an era, for with the coming of a

---

[23]Faulkner, p. 314.

lumber company, ridding the land of its timber, change is apparent everywhere. Ike's one consolation now comes from his knowledge of the unity of the wilderness, for in the earth of the woods where Sam, Lion, and Old Ben lay buried they have all become as one:

> not held fast in earth but free in earth and not in earth but of earth, myriad yet undiffused of every myriad part, leaf and twig and particle, air and sun and rain and dew and night, acorn oak and leaf and acorn again, dark and dawn and dark and dawn again in their immutable progression and, being myriad, one. (pp. 328-29)

This final symbolic and poetically beautiful expression of the meaning of primal unity as realized through the sporting myth is dramatically contrasted with the actions of Boon Hogganbeck, who, in his selfish attempt to assemble his gun in time to kill the squirrels swarming in the tree above him, symbolizes the warped outlook of the rules-breaker, which imprisons rather than frees, suggesting man's absurd belief that he "owns" the wilderness.

So we observe that Ike McCaslin's encounter experience, as realized through the ritual of the "best game of all," enables him to transcend the inherent evils of society, while his renunciation of material wealth affords him the opportunity to forge his own meaning of personal freedom. For this alone, Ike McCaslin rises above his symbolic role in the sporting myth to stand as one of the most positive characters in all modern fiction.

Santiago: The Meaning of Value in Defeat

"But man is not made for defeat," he said. "A man can be destroyed but not defeated."
—Hemingway, *The Old Man and the Sea*

Ihab Hassan has observed that the greatest American writers create values out of defeat, and because of this achievement "reality can be redeemed."[24] Faulkner is an obvious example of this insight, since Ike McCaslin in his quest to distinguish between illusion and reality sacrifices his worldly gains to effect a personal sense of victory. An even more outstanding example of this theme in American literature is Ernest Hemingway's marvelous old fisherman, Santiago of *The Old Man and the Sea* (1952). Like Ike, Santiago also practices a code of self-denial and renunciation, exemplified by his act of going beyond what is normally expected of not only an old fisherman but any fisherman. But whereas the central conflict in Ike's encounter is precipitated by what he learns about life from the ritual of the hunt, the meaning of Santiago's encounter grows out of the conflict within his own mind concerning whether to stay within or to go beyond the bounds set for fishermen. Santiago's defiance of the so-called limitations of man reminds us of the athlete's competitive sense, and although he feels that his impossible quest may be the cause of his poor luck, his courage and endurance in facing the task before him remind us also that Santiago, in undergoing his experience of encounter, creates a sense of victory out of defeat.

The concept of "essential encounter" is present in most of the writings of Hemingway because his "drama almost always turns on some principle of courage, of pity, of honor—in short, of sportsmanship, in its largest sense."[25] Thus Hemingway appears to be at his best when he depicts a one-to-one confrontation of experience, in which the "essential encounter" is realized

---

[24]Ihab Hassam, *Radical Innocence: Studies in the Contemporary American Novel* (Princeton University Press, 1961), p. 55.

[25]Edmund Wilson, "The Sportsman's Tragedy," *The Shores of Light* (New York: Farrar, Straus, and Cudahy, 1952), p. 341.

through dramatic rendering of the metaphor of the game—the bullfight, the hunt, the fishing contest—even war itself. In such events it is the quality of performance that measures the worth of the individual involved; accordingly, Hemingway's art is concerned with the war or struggle being waged within a man's inner being when undergoing such a test. One of the best of the earlier stories dramatizing this concept of "essential encounter" is "The Short and Happy Life of Francis Macomber." Macomber, intimidated and cuckolded by his aggressive wife (again the feminine principle is denigrated), realizes that his manhood is at stake unless, of course, he can redeem himself through a courageous act on the hunt. It is as though, as Arthur Mizener puts it, Macomber is being "confronted by one of those occasions that constitute reality and call forth our essential moral natures."[26]

Macomber, like the other Hemingway heroes, is confronted with a moral problem because the encounter always calls into question the individual's integrity in terms of his courage and endurance. Thus the Hemingway heroes face a test that demands an athletic performance to project a self-sufficient image in the face of what seems superior odds, and

> even though Hemingway's heroes are in a sense, winners who take nothing, they *are* winners and the manner of their taking is individually self-generated, within situations largely of their own choosing, and under circumstances in which their native resources for physical action and courage are given every possibility of espression.[27]

The phrase of one critic, "morality in action,"[28] then, is an apt one to apply to the central experience of a

[26]Arthur Mizener, *The Sense of Life in the Modern Novel* (Boston: Houghton Mifflin Co., 1964), p. 226.

[27]Earl Rovit, *Ernest Hemingway* (New York: Twayne, 1963), p. 25.

[28]James B. Colvert, "Ernest Hemingway's Morality in Action," *American Literature* 27 (November 1955): 376.

Hemingway story in the tradition of the sporting myth, since solution to the moral question of the story is so dependent on the quality of the hero's action. For example, even the paradox of Nick Adams's retreat in "Big Two-Hearted River" is morally significant, because passive action here is equated with the meaningful activity of fishing, one of the good things of Nick's past that helps him to forget the horrors of war and forge his own "separate peace." Treatment of forest and stream as the sanctified "good place" is stressed throughout the story and contrasted with the "burned out" world surrounding Nick's retreat:

> Ahead of him, as far as he could see, was the pine plain. The burned country stopped off at the left with the range of hills. On ahead islands of dark pine trees rose out of the plain. Far off to the left was the line of the river. Nick followed it with his eye and caught glints of the water in the sun.[29]

Even in the much longer work, *The Sun Also Rises* (1926), Jake's pastoral retreat to woods and stream in the Spanish Pyrenees is integral to the overall purpose of the novel and symbolizes the hero's inherent desire to forsake the societal ties of the city (Paris) and return to the simpler time of childhood innocence for reaffirmation, perhaps even rebirth.

Underlying the retreat concept in "Big Two-Hearted River" is the germ for the dramatization of the big fish that got away, an important metaphor for understanding works like *The Old Man and the Sea* and *Islands in the Stream* (1970) because it expresses so well Hemingway's personal code of winning by losing. After Nick loses his trout, Hemingway writes:

[29]Hemingway, *Short Stories*, p. 211.

He thought of the trout somewhere on the bottom, holding himself steady over the gravel, far down below the light, under the logs, with the hook in his jaw. Nick knew the trout's teeth would cut through the snell of the hook. The hook would imbed itself in his jaw. He'd bet the trout was angry. Anything that size would be angry. That was a trout. He had been solidly hooked. Solid as a rock. He felt like a rock, too, before he started off. By God, he was a big one. By God, he was the biggest one I·ever heard of. (p. 226-27)

Already evident in this passage is the fisherman's sense of awe and respect for having confronted such a mysterious and huge adversary. The feeling will evolve and express itself most magnificently in Santiago's trials with his big fish.

Some note should perhaps be made of the reason for Nick's lack of initiative in wanting to fish the dark swampy area of the stream for big fish, because such an attitude appears contradictory to the Hemingway code as it relates to the sporting myth. Toward the end of the story Nick expresses his antipathy toward the swamp: "He felt a reaction against deep wading with the water deepening up under his armpits, to hook big trout in places impossible to land them" (p. 231). Nick's reticence can be explained through his role as the type of sporting hero who, in directly and fully relating to nature, feels no compulsion to undergo the encounter experience. In this story Nick's whole purpose is to relate to nature through the retreat concept. In other fiction dealing with heroes of urbanized background, the retreat to nature can never be realized because societal demands present obstacles. Nick has obviously cut all these off, and in his story of pure retreat there can be no test or trial to be undergone. Thus the closing line of the story ("There were plenty of days coming when he could fish the swamp") anticipates the encounter experiences of Nick's later life.

In other experiences of Nick Adams we can observe multiple characteristics of the sporting myth operative, even as early as the story "Indian Camp," which subtly reinforces the sporting hero's dream of immortality. Having witnessed the Indian who had killed himself with a razor because of his wife's sickness in childbirth, Nick, an innocent who has been in the presence of death, is moved to reflect on the way home: "In the early morning on the lake sitting on the stern of the boat with his father rowing, he felt quite sure that he would never die" (p. 95). At the close of "The Doctor and the Doctor's Wife," Nick's decision to go with his father rather than see his mother reveals his natural affinity for the outdoors as opposed to the home and its restrictive, sterile existence, symbolized by Nick's mother in bed with the blinds drawn. It is pertinent to our definition of the sporting myth that Nick learns all the basics of living in the woods, certainly not at home.

In two companion pieces, "The End of Something" and "The Three Day Blow," the sportsman's ambivalent attitude toward woman is brought out through Nick's breakup with his girl, Marjorie. An idyllic trip trolling for trout comes to an abrupt end when Nick informs Marjorie that their relationship "isn't fun anymore." In "The Three Day Blow" we learn why. In the masculine world of a cottage in the wilderness, Nick and his friend Bill drink and discuss baseball, literature, and the necessity for his breakup with Marjorie. Bill says:

> "It was the only thing to do. If you hadn't by now you'd be back home working trying to get enough money to get married."
> Nick said nothing.
> "Once a man's married he's absolutely bitched," Bill went on. "He hasn't got anything more. Nothing. Not a damn

thing. He's done for. You've seen the guys that get mar-
ried."
　　Nick said nothing.
"You can tell them," Bill said. "They get this sort of fat
married look. They're done for."
　　"Sure," said Nick. (p. 122)

But Nick's noncommital attitude vanishes when they get
the guns and head for the point. He thinks: "Outside
now the Marge business was no longer so tragic. It was
not even very important. The wind blew everything like
that away" (p. 125). Involvement with nature frees the
sporting character from societal ties.

　　Again fear of loss of personal freedom through involvement with woman is forcefully presented in
"Soldier's Home," in the attitude of Krebs, who is really
another Nick Adams returned from the war. Hemingway observes:

> Nothing was changed in the town except that the young
> girls had grown up. But they lived in such a complicated
> world of already defined alliances and shifting feuds that
> Krebs did not feel the energy or the courage to break into
> it. (p. 147)

The entire story exists as the intense statement of an individual set upon keeping his life style simple and un-
committed. Girls are obstacles to this end because they
are too "complicated." In other words, "the world they
were in was not the world he was in" (p. 148), a life free
of consequences.

　　This attitude toward woman is enhanced by the role
of the mother, who reminds Krebs of his failure in ful-
filling a societal function by not getting married, settling
down, and becoming "a credit to the community." Overall, it is the stifling atmosphere of the home that repres-

ses Krebs, and he realizes that he must leave it if he is to fulfill self. It is significant that the only person in the story he identifies with is an innocent, his little sister who likes to play baseball.

The story "Fathers and Sons" reveals that sex can be meaningful for the sporting figure if the act is equated with nature, as when Nick discovers sexual fulfillment with an Indian girl in the Michigan woods. His relationship with her is natural, free, and uninhibited. In Nick's words, "she did first what no one has ever done better" (p. 497). Nick's open attitude toward sex is contrasted with his father's puritanical, restrictive one, an outlook that brands him a prisoner of society even while enjoying the freedom of the woods.

Other works in the Hemingway canon reiterate inherent characteristics of the sporting hero. The story of Manuel, the aging bullfighter, in "The Undefeated" is really the story of Santiago in another time, another place. As a test of the meaning of courage and endurance, the one-to-one ritual of the bullfight translates admirably into the requisites for success in the world of big-game fishing. In *Islands in the Stream* Thomas Hudson revitalizes his own compartmentalized life through his son's initiation into manhood by pursuing a big fish. Hudson's catharsis is akin to that of a spectator watching and identifying with the performance of his favorite player. To his other son's concern over David's ordeal in trying to land the huge swordfish, Hudson responds: "But please know I would have stopped this long ago except that I know that if David catches this fish he'll have something inside him for all his life and it will make everything else easier."[30] One begins to face life when he faces struggle or even death, Hudson implies.

[30]Ernest Hemingway, *Islands in the Stream* (New York: Charles Scribner's Sons, 1970), p. 131.

An important clue to understanding the sporting figure's relationship with nature is brought out when David, after losing his big fish, relates to the others who have witnessed his struggle:

> "In the worst parts, when I was the tiredest I couldn't tell which was him and which was me."
> "I understand," Roger said.
> "Then I began to love him more than anything on earth."
> "You mean really love him?" Andrew asked.
> "Yeah. Really love him."
> "Gee," said Andrew. "I can't understand that."
> "I loved him so much when I saw him coming up that I couldn't stand it," David said, his eyes still shut. "All I wanted was to see him closer."[31]

Extending one's self through involvement in nature or "the game" is an important step toward self-discovery in the literature of the sporting myth. Ironically, participants in a contest fight each other only to help each other, and the intimacy that grows out of a struggle of this order is what enables a participant to reevaluate self in the light of his performance. The desire to "see . . . closer" is really the same impulse that impels Ike to look upon Old Ben and drives Santiago out beyond the limits of the average fisherman to achieve self-knowledge. Such a quest, in placing emphasis on the quality of an action expended to achieve a goal rather than on the act of achieving the goal itself, expresses the measure of the man through his performance and not necessarily through his accomplishment. The one work of Hemingway that best symbolizes this version of the essential encounter is *The Old Man and the Sea*.

In this story of an old Cuban fisherman who has gone eighty-four days without a catch, the merit of the action

[31]*Ibid.*, pp. 142-43.

is continually being played off against the obstacles that exist to be overcome. To heighten this intention, Hemingway begins by painting a vividly humble picture of Santiago. He is stripped of those common material possessions that most people take for granted. Even his skiff, the most essential thing he owns, is described as having a sail that "was patched with flour sacks and, furled, it looked like the flag of permanent defeat."[32]

The shirt he wears has a similar appearance, but the old man's exterior appearance serves to enhance his individuality and the simple Spartan life that has always been integral to the romantic conception of the sporting hero. Like Natty Bumppo, the old man has learned to live without the luxuries of life, and his years against the sea have taught him many lessons in the meaning of humility. As Hemingway expresses it: "He was too simple to wonder when he had attained humility. But he knew he had attained it and he knew it was not disgraceful and it carried no loss of true pride" (pp. 13-14). The lesson here is the same one Ike McCaslin learned through the ritual of the hunt—that true humility grows out of a self-effacing attitude toward life.

As Faulkner's favorite word is *endurance*, so Hemingway's is *undefeated,* the personification of which is the various heroes that appear throughout the Hemingway canon, culminating most forcibly in the character of Santiago. But to be "undefeated," one must possess endurance. Ike McCaslin as a young person best symbolizes the fact that the quality of endurance is something that must be acquired; on the other hand, Santiago, the old man, is the very symbol of that acquired endurance which enables him to come through

[32]Ernest Hemingway, *The Old Man and the Sea* (New York: Scribner Library, 1952). p. 9.

undefeated, and without which heroic realization is impossible. Santiago, then, is really Ike grown old.

Throughout the story Santiago refers to a hero of modern organized sport, Joe DiMaggio, who is an individualized sporting figure with whom he can identify since, in the latter years of his baseball career, DiMaggio suffered a heel injury that hampered his playing. Despite the injury he still managed to perform marvelous feats on the field. Thus when the old man tells the boy Manolin to think of the great DiMaggio, he is reminding him that he too must learn endurance in the manner that Sam Fathers reminds Ike of his obligation to the wilderness. Even when the New York Yankees lose, it is DiMaggio who "makes the difference" on the Yankee team because, whether they win or lose, he remains a symbol of the undefeated in Santiago's eyes.

During his encounter with the big fish, the old man sustains himself from time to time by thinking on the example the American athlete has set: "I must have confidence and I must be worthy of the great DiMaggio who does all things perfectly even with the pain of the bone spur in his heel" (p. 68). The bone spur, ostensibly a sign of weakness, becomes for Santiago a symbol of strength, and a reason for further comparison of himself with his baseball idol: "Do you believe the great DiMaggio would stay with a fish as long as I will stay with this one? he thought. I am sure he would and more. . . . Also his father was a fisherman" (p. 68). The fact that Santiago identifies with the wounded hero of a game like baseball is appropriate to his situation because baseball is a game that stresses individual performance within an interdependent sphere of action. Important to the understanding of this story, too, is that the old man's relationship with nature is interdependent. Thus Joe DiMaggio's predicament is really that of Santiago's as it expresses itself through team sports. Even after he has killed the great fish, Santiago refers again to his hero: " 'I think the great DiMaggio would be proud of me today. I had no bone spurs. But the hands and the back hurt truly.' I wonder what a bone spur is, he thought. Maybe we have them without knowing of it" (p. 97). Santiago's experience teaches that even though the individual may have a particular weakness, it can be overcome by drawing on one's inner resources to face adversity and grow in self-esteem. Thus Santiago's encounter with the marlin, from his first being towed out to sea to his eventual return to port with only the fish's skeleton, becomes more than a contest between man and fish. It is a journey toward self-discovery, and the marlin as a part of the interdependent scheme of nature teaches Santiago more about self than anything else he confronts.

As Old Ben and the ritual of the hunt existed to educate Ike McCaslin in the ways of the woods and, by extension, in the meaning of endurance, so the marlin tests Santiago's understanding of what it means to endure. Rather than being a deterrent, the size of the fish both awes and encourages the old man, and he swears to kill the fish "in all his greatness and his glory," a common oath that obsesses all romantic conceptions of the sporting myth: to kill or defeat that which they instinctively love. Like the bear in the hunt, the fish is both feared and venerated because he helps to remind Santiago what a man must go through to endure. In Hemingway's metaphor of the bullfight, the interrelationship of man and beast is utilized to show the triumph of the matador as symbolizing man's sense of pride in confronting and overcoming the most adamant of adversaries, death itself. Similarly, the intimate relationship of man and fish in this story underscores the necessity for a sense of pride in man's ability to endure whatever the natural forces around him may have in store, even the threat of annihilation. It is a paradoxical lesson, because the old fisherman learns just as much from identifying with the pursued as being the pursuer—the lesson that David learns from his fight with the giant fish in *Islands in the Stream.* This attitude asserts itself at the beginning when Santiago expresses pity for the "wonderful and strange" fish he has hooked, and their interdependence is emphasized when the old man addresses the fish: "I love you and respect you very much. But I will kill you dead before this very day ends" (p. 54). In the world of sport such an attitude is not uncommon. It is manifest among players competing for the same position; it expresses itself in the love-hate relationship of player and coach; and any time a college football team boasts it will defeat its Saturday opponent, it implies a sense of respect for that team. We shall see that there are other implications in this outlook as well.

The size of the hunted always impresses the hunter, and the immensity of the marlin ("two feet longer than the skiff") enhances both its symbolic import and the old man's respect for it: "I must never let him learn his strength nor what he could do if he made his run" (p. 63). The fish must be caught within the rules set for the pursuit, and the old man's identity with the fish during the chase increases his respect for him as he reflects: "I wish I was the fish . . . with everything he has against only my will and my intelligence" (p. 64). But the fish, lacking these human characteristics, is a creature that achieves a kind of nobility through testing Santiago's endurance. In doing so it becomes apparent that both man and fish represent complementary sides of the same thing—what it takes to achieve a position of honor and dignity. Thus each side is no more the master than the other is, a situation symbolically expressed in the old man's wondering, when he is towing the dead fish into port, whether he was bringing the fish in or the fish was bringing him in: "they were sailing together lashed side by side and the old man thought, let him bring me in if it pleases him. I am only better than him through trickery and he meant me no harm" (p. 99). Even within the "rules," Santiago has the upper hand, but the fish nevertheless has left his mark on the old man.

In this story the role of suffering and pain plays an essential part. In fact, a reason for suffering is one important aspect arising out of the story's central encounter itself, for *The Old Man and the Sea* is probably the finest dramatization of the fact that "Hemingway's ultimate test of human performance is the degree of stripped courage and dignity which man can discover in himself in his moments of absolute despair."[33] One incident in the story illustrates how Santiago's understanding of the meaning of pain has changed since his youth, the time in Casablanca when he passed one day and one night hand-wrestling a Negro, "the strongest man on the docks." Even though the young Santiago defeated the black, he respected him in the manner of the sporting hero as "a fine man and a great athlete," and because of this experience he learned an important lesson in enduring without complaint. But one of the reasons he decided to give up the matches was that "it was bad for his right hand for fishing." How different is his attitude when now as an old man he injures his hand in attempting to restrain the giant fish: "It is not bad," he said. "And pain does not matter to a man." Christlike, he is now aware of pain only as it affects others. Observe his feelings even toward the fish: "I must hold his pain where it is. . . . Mine does not matter. I can control mine. But his pain could drive him mad."[34] As a romantic type of the

[33]Rovit, p. 63.
[34]Hemingway, *The Old Man and the Sea*, p. 88.

sporting myth, Santiago is sensitive to the feelings of any creature around him. His outlook markedly contrasts with that of the urbanized neo-romantic type who, because of his inability to assess self, is impervious to the feelings of those around him.

Other sporting myth traits manifest themselves when the old man is attempting to bring the marlin in to port. At a critical moment he calls on God to help him endure, but his act is more an imploration than it is a justification of his belief in a Power beyond himself. In fact, organized religion suggests to him the concept of sin, of which he, as an innocent type, has no comprehension and in which he is not sure he can believe:

> Perhaps it was a sin to kill the fish. I suppose it was even though I did it to keep me alive and feed many people. But then everything is a sin. Do not think about sin. It is much too late for that and there are people who are paid to do it. Let them think about it. . . .
>
>   You did not kill the fish only to keep alive and sell for food, he thought. You killed him for pride and because you are a fisherman. You loved him when he was alive and you loved him after. If you love him, it is not a sin to kill him. (p. 105)

Santiago's rationalization is a result of the conflict between his own natural impulses and the restrictions of an institution. Such a conflict contributes to the distorted behavior of the sporting figure with a background in organized sport who is divorced from a natural environment as is Rabbit Angstrom and whose erratic experience is in part influenced by the dictates of organized religion. Like his ancestor Natty Bumppo, the modern sporting hero still reflects a sensitivity to the imposition of society's institutions, but usually there is no avenue of escape open to him.

The most outstanding characteristic of the sporting

myth reflected in the old man's experience is, of course,
the belief that the power to overcome a barrier does not
lie outside the self but within it—hence Santiago's supreme faith in the sacredness of his own ability to act
heroically against the problems that beset him, in order
to achieve dignity, honor, and self-knowledge. His faith
is that of the athlete magnificently confident of winning
against all odds. Thus his persistent demand that his
body endure the physical ordeal of his quest: "Pull,
hands, he thought. Hold up, legs. Last for me, head.
Last for me" (p. 91). The individual must assess the privacy of his own experience to "know how to suffer like a
man." For Santiago the confrontation with the great fish
is an essential and complementary part of this assessment.

In going beyond what is normally expected of an old
fisherman, then, Santiago makes a choice that labels his
experience as unique as a champion athlete's. Although
he could have chosen to remain within reasonable limits
and attain a good catch, the old man decides to pursue
the great fish he has hooked and measure his own
heroic potential. It is a decision that improves the quality
of performance and defines the meaning of encounter
in this work, for in an ultimate sense Santiago's struggle
with the giant marlin symbolizes the necessity for man's
"going beyond" to realize his true worth. Accordingly,
there is a direct identity with the fish whose

> choice had been to stay in the deep dark water far out
> beyond all snares and traps and treacheries. My choice was
> to go there to find him beyond all people. Beyond all peo-
> ple in the world. Now we are joined together. . . . And no
> one to help either one of us. (p. 50)

It is such knowledge that increases the determination of
the old man and urges him to stay with the fish until the

creature is dead. Thus Santiago's peculiar kind of isolation leads to further definition of self. Now he does not
even have the boy to comfort him. There are only the
fish, himself, and the sea.

In this story in which no major women characters appear, the sea, *la mar*, is always thought by the old man to
have a feminine nature. She is not only kind and very
beautiful in her own way, but sometimes cruel, and "if
she did wild or wicked things it was because she could
not help them. The moon affects her as it does a
woman, he thought" (p. 30). Here again is evidence of
the special attitude toward the feminine principle that all
works related to the sporting myth reflect. Its use here
enhances the significance of the sea as a character in the
story, and gives Hemingway an effective means of
dramatizing the triumph of masculine integrity over
feminine duplicity. It is a victory that does not occur too
often in literature of the sporting myth.

Another obstacle helps to reinforce the ultimate meaning of Santiago's story. In confronting the sharks that
will eventually devour his fish, the old man, like the athlete who has tried too hard, reminds himself that perhaps
his luck has been violated because he has gone "too far
outside." If anything has beaten him, he intimates, it is
the fact that he has not stayed within the normal limits.
Paradoxically, though, it is this trespassing of the outer
limits that makes of him a victorious figure even in defeat. In his Nobel Literary Prize speech in 1954,
Hemingway made the clearest statement in explanation
of this paradox when he evaluated the writer's goals in
terms of an athleticlike quest:

> For a true writer, each book should be a new beginning
> where he tries again for something that is beyond attain-
> ment. He should always try for something that has never
> been done or that others have tried and failed.... It is be-

cause we have had such great writers in the past that a writer is driven far out past where he can go, out to where no one can help him.

No one, that is, except those inner resources that self must draw upon to overcome whatever obstacles might exist in the way toward a goal. Thus, after beating off all the scavenging sharks, even though they leave him nothing but the skeleton of his fish, Santiago arrives back in port alone, with the knowledge that he had made a choice and stuck to it—a quality of action that designates the old man as truly "undefeated."

The tourists at the end of the story who mistake the carcass of the great marlin for that of a shark illustrate the distorted perception of those who have never undergone the experience of "going beyond." As societal figures they are truly limited, and in their vision of mistaken values, they are really the "defeated" ones. This final incident thus stands as both an attack on the self-limiting attitude of modern life and a tribute to the worth and dignity of the individual as represented in Santiago's manner of searching these qualities out. The real significance of Santiago's encounter at sea is that it imparts meaning and value to an existence that would otherwise seem abortive.

3

Encounter with Society

Introduction

In contrast to the sporting hero who comes to a realization of self through encounter with or "within" nature, the hero who expresses himself through the organized sport of modern society finds self-discovery a difficult and frustrating ordeal, simply because a society or a system represents a world alien to the natural innocence that is the true heritage of the sporting hero. Like his brother who confronts nature, the figure who becomes involved in society cannot fathom the civilized world of woman, and in his intense desire to be a part of the action, those positive characteristics he inherited from Natty Bumppo become distorted. We see, then, that this variety of the sporting myth has much in common with Washington Irving's archetypal Brom Bones, who, in his desire to maintain status, is fearful that the outsider may destroy his image as well as his ideal situation.

The characters examined in this section all profess this fear, either consciously or subconsciously. Jack Keefe of Ring Lardner's *You Know Me Al,* is a big-league pitcher, but first of all he is a small-town boy come to the big city. Jack is a competent player on the field, but in the hostile world of the city he moves from social blunder to social fiasco while never once realizing the implication of his actions, a fact that emphatically adds to our understanding of his basically innocent nature. To preserve his own image, Jack is given to lying and futile attempts at convincing himself of his secure status. As a result the overall portrait of Jack Keefe approaches caricature; at the same time, we observe brilliant flashes of Ring Lardner's perceptiveness in analyzing human nature. Jack Keefe, then, is a variant of the traditional sporting hero in that he is compelled to distort a code of behavior for the sake of self-security.

Both Nelson Algren's Lefty Bicek of *Never Come Morning* and James Jones's Robert E. Lee Prewitt of *From Here to Eternity* are boxers who have significant relationships with the fight game. The experience of both heroes is presented so that not only each character's attitude toward life is brought out but also the inherent defects of a society or system. But while Lefty sees boxing as a means of escaping the delimiting confines of the city slums, Prewitt defiantly quits boxing in order to realize identity in the vast impersonal system of the U.S. Army. In such writing, in which the hero is powerless within the web of society or system, literary technique is controlled by naturalistic expression.

The fact that success in athletics does not always mean success in business or life provides Philip Roth in *Goodbye, Columbus* and Irwin Shaw in "The Eighty-Yard Run" with a convenient means for satirical expression. We discover that Roth's Ron Patimkin and Shaw's Christian Darling as ex-college athletes are unable to involve themselves with the realities of life. Instead, they continue to live in the idealized world of "the game"; consequently their lives exemplify still another theme in modern literature—the search for maturity.

In this section, then, the sporting hero's encounter with society reveals his intense desire to relate himself to a freer, more natural environment. But paradoxically his intent is doomed to failure because the innocent, self-expressive nature of the fictional character tempered by the sporting myth cannot freely assert itself in a man-made society.

Jack Keefe and the Code of the Busher

> Well Al it will seem funny to be up there in the big show when I never was really in the big city before. But I guess I seen enough of life not to be scared of the high buildings eh Al?
>
> —Ring Lardner, *You Know Me Al*

Ring Lardner did not look upon the athlete as a special breed. Instead, he saw him as all too human, and his delineation of an athlete's personal faults shows his universal understanding of people in all their pettiness and meanness. In his baseball pitcher, Jack Keefe, he has created a character at once recognizable, partly because he is a ballplayer, but mainly because he is a human being. Donald Elder, Lardner's biographer, observes that for all his faults Jack is "not unlikable. He is not very much worse than anyone else; he is real. He is not quite like yourself, but he bears a fatal resemblance to your friends."[1] Such a tribute is indicative not only of Lardner's power of expression but of his genius for synthesizing in one figure the defects of an increasingly urbanized society in pursuit of material values in the early part of this century. The remarkable thing is that Lardner had the audacity to choose an honored folk-hero type to project his feelings about the course the

[1] Donald Elder, *Ring Lardner* (Garden City: Doubleday & Co., 1956), p. 114.

American people were taking. The game of baseball has always held a place of reverence among American institutions, and as recently as 1969, when ex-player Jim Bouton published his *Ball Four*—a supposedly nonfictional account of life in the big leagues, much criticism was leveled at the author for revealing many of the game's superplayers as human beings with faults and weaknesses like anyone else.

Before *You Know Me Al* (1916) began to appear in serial form in *The Saturday Evening Post* in 1914, the image of the athlete, particularly that of the baseball player, was a sacred thing. He was a composite of many of the qualities the American people revered most, a true modern counterpart of the frontier folk hero, that great "innocent" who called forth all his resourcefulness and know-how to defeat whatever his "antagonist," the frontier, had to throw his way. But by deglamorizing the athlete and undermining the Frank Merriwell myth, Lardner exhibited the prophetic vein of the true satirist and saw an end to the innocence that characterized the American people before the First World War. One has only to compare the sophisticated manner of a baseball player of today, a Johnny Bench type, for example, with the crude air of Lardner's busher, Jack Keefe, to conclude that baseball as an indigenous American sport has come a long way.

In choosing such a character as Jack as a symbol, though, Lardner was depicting a subtle kind of uneasiness that was settling upon the American people before World War I. Essentially it was a feeling generated by a nation in transition from an agrarian to an urban society. We sense this feeling of transition as underlying part of Jack Keefe's makeup, for he is a country boy who has come to the city because of his ability at playing a game; and even though he tries to "make it big" in cities like Washington, New York, and Chicago, the contrast between these places and his home town of Bedford, Indiana, is too great for him to overcome. Lardner's epistolary structural device containing Jack's illiterate and childlike deficiencies in English expression exists as a perpetual reminder that Jack has never really left home. Urgently in need of a confidant, someone whom he obviously cannot find in city life. Jack writes innumerable letters to his buddy Al back in Bedford. This urgent need to confide in someone is the most telling thing about Jack's basic insecurity and results in his painting an unsparing but unknowing portrait of himself. At times Jack's naïveté seems almost unbelievable, but Lardner's skill in portraying human relationships redeems the apparent absurdity of most situations, as in the following:

> Friend Al: Coming out of Amarillo last night I and Lord and Weaver was sitting at a table in the dining car with a old lady. None of us were talking to her but she looked me over pretty careful and seemed to kind of like my looks. Finally she says Are you boys with some football club? Lord nor Weaver didn't say nothing so I thought it was up to me and I says No mam this is the Chicago White Sox Ball Club. She says I knew you were athaletes. I says Yes I guess you could spot us for athaletes. She says Yes indeed and specially you. You certainly look healthy. I says You ought to see me stripped. I didn't see nothing funny about that but I thought Lord and Weaver would die laughing. Lord had to get up and leave the table and he told everybody what I said.[2]

In Jack's case the narcissistic side of the sporting hero forces him into countless social blunders and distorted assessments of himself. In reporting a faux pas to "Friend Al," he does so in a tone of voice that is not

<hr/>

[2]Ring Lardner, *You Know Me Al* (New York: Charles Scribner's Sons, 1960), pp. 36-37.

only unaware but apparently dismayed that anyone would not see things his way. One might say that the art of making excuses is Jack Keefe's greatest talent. Note his reaction to losing his first start against Detroit:

> Dear Old Pal: Well Al it's just as well you couldn't come. They beat me and I am writing you this so as you will know the truth about the game and not get a bum steer from what you read in the papers.
>
> I had a sore arm when I was warming up and Callahan should never ought to of sent me in there. . . . Weaver and Lord and all of them kept kicking them round the infield and Collins and Bodie couldn't catch nothing.
>
> Callahan ought never to of left me in there when he seen how sore my arm was. Why, I couldn't of threw hard enough to break a pain of glass my arm was so sore. (p. 44)

Jack makes excuses because his peculiar kind of self-centeredness grows out of his inability to relate his rural background to the urbanized life of a big leaguer. The great disparity between two different ways of life forces Jack into unnatural reactions and assessments of his predicament. In many such stories, country shrewdness usually wins out over city "slickness," but not so with Jack. As an innocent person bewildered by the ways of the big city, he would probably be much better off if he would pack up and head back to Bedford. But like the competitor he is, he remains, still hoping to succeed while staying continually on the defensive and stumbling through a never-ending series of social misunderstandings. In practicing his paranoid ethics in an alien society, Jack Keefe projects an image of the small-mindedness and self-indulgence of a class of people in search of itself—those whom Lardner termed "bushers," or a people who lack the perceptiveness to evaluate the real circumstances surrounding themselves. Motivated by mat-

erial success, the "busher" never loses sight of the dream
of making it big.

You Know Me Al, then, is much more than a work in
the American vernacular tradition. It is the first meaningful example in American literature of what happens
when the sporting hero comes to the city. His sense of
values distorted because of the antipathy between his
more natural background and the artificiality of his urbanized existence, the literary hero of organized sport
becomes a distortion himself. In contrast to the heroes
who identify with nature, represented in chapter 2
above, Jack Keefe is totally unable to pursue any self-
effacing code of behavior; instead he is preoccupied
with pursuing his own selfish ends in order to improve
his image. In short, Jack Keefe is everything that Natty
Bumppo is not, for he continually deceives himself with
the belief that he is "in" with his strange, new environment when in reality he is "out." The tension that results
from Jack's inability to come to terms with self and perceive situation controls the art of *You Know Me Al.* In a
larger sense this atmosphere of tension is generated by
Jack's failure to cope with his experience of "encounter,"
that is, his ineptness in coping with the demands of society. Jack Keefe's problem has been aptly expressed as
follows:

> Jack is an innocent moving in a highly competitive world,
> and he impotently strives to make this world appreciate his
> true worth, but it continually rejects his self-created image
> and perpetually thwarts his best efforts.[3]

Jack's naïveté about his rejection, however, is indicative
of Lardner's sure use of irony to reveal his major con-

[3]Walton R. Patrick, *Ring Lardner* (New York: Twayne, 1963), p. 46.

cern: the difference between the real and the ideal. The choice of an athlete with an overwhelming ignorance of his shortcomings to convey the theme of alienation was an ingenious conception on the part of Lardner. If Jack Keefe may be termed an unreliable narrator in regard to the externalities of his world, he is more than reliable in unwittingly revealing the truth about himself; for "the image of himself that Jack unconsciously presents to Al and the reader is . . . the reverse of the one he has of himself."[4] Al, of course, is the straight man to Jack's personal obsessions; yet we feel that whether he sees through Jack or not, his most important function in the book is that of a father figure who can absorb the subconscious uncertainties that haunt such a person as the "busher."

In another sense Lardner's character study is similar to Sherwood Anderson's incisive portraits of people pursuing the Success Myth of the twenties. Anderson called his characters "grotesques," because they are warped for lack of love and as a result are continually trying to be something they are not. These are also figures who are beginning to feel the pressures created by the shift from an agrarian society to one that is predominantly urban. Lardner, however, in portraying his characteristic understanding of the pursuit of success, chose the perfect background metaphor in "the game." Although Jack can salvage some modicum of self-esteem because of his achievements on the baseball diamond, he courts disaster in his private life.

In convincingly dramatizing Jack Keefe's inability to respond to the social demands of the city, Lardner emphasizes the fact that Jack is a failure in three main areas of experience, all of them thrust on him by his immersion into city life: money problems, lack of inner

[4]*Ibid.*, p. 45.

security, and a catastrophic relationship with women. With his status as a big league ballplayer, he has more money, but he is unsure as to how to spend it. At first his uncertainty seems a part of his rural innocence, as he reveals when he first gets to New York:

> Al I told you Boston was some town but this is the real one. I never seen nothing like it and I been going some since we got here. I walked down Broadway the Main Street last night and I run into a couple of the ball players and they took me to what they call the Garden but it ain't like the gardens at home because this one is indoors. We sat down to a table and had several drinks. Pretty soon one of the boys asked me if I was broke and I says No, why? He says You better get some lubricating oil and loosen up. I don't know what he meant but pretty soon when we had a lot of drinks the waiter brings a check and hands it to me. It was for one dollar. I says Oh I ain't paying for all of them. The waiter says This is just for that last drink.
>
> I thought the other boys would make a holler but they didn't say nothing. So I give him a dollar bill and even then he didn't act satisfied so I asked him what he was waiting for and he said Oh nothing, kind of sassy.[5]

Actually Jack's tightness with money is closely related to his feelings of insecurity, and we observe that the more involved Jack becomes with the ways of society, the more his penurious manner is transformed into a kind of suspicious arrogance. After his marriage to Florrie he itemizes the cost of the wedding for Al:

> You see Al it costs a hole lot of money to get married here. The sum of what I wrote down is $29.40 but as I told you I have spent $30 and I do not know what I have did with the other $0.60. My new brother-in-law Allen told me I should ought to give the preist $5 and I thought it should be about $2 the same as the license so I split the difference and give him $3.50. I never seen him before and probably won't

[5]Lardner, pp. 65-66.

never see him again so why should I give him anything at all when it is his business to marry couples? But I like to do the right thing. You know me Al. (p. 84)

The "right thing" to Jack, of course, is always the wrong thing according to what is socially accepted. His marriage is just the beginning of his financial woes, for Florrie turns out to be a spendthrift who drags the unsuspecting Jack deeply into debt. In order to extricate himself from his predicament he is forced to borrow money from Al, an act in itself symbolic of Jack's desire to identify with a more reliable source than that which he encounters in the city.

Also closely related to Jack's lack of inner security is his penchant for self-indulgence, a situation that expresses itself periodically. After one of his holdout periods he rejoins the White Sox and meets a trainer who asks,

Are you in shape? And I told him Yes I am. He says Yes you look in shape like a barrel. I says They is not no fat on me and if I am a little bit bigger than last year it is because my mussels is bigger. He says Yes your stumach mussels is emense and you must of gave them plenty of exercise. (p. 127)

Psychologically, Jack's tendency to overeat plays a key part in his readjustment to the team and city life, almost as though he is seeking reassurance from a familiar source about his shaky position. But this kind of identification leads only to further self-deception and the inevitable excuses for breaking the social code.

One of Ring Lardner's baseball stories is entitled "Alibi Ike" (1915), an important story in the Lardner canon because implicit within it is Lardner's understanding of human behavior as an entrapment in the social structure and search for the path of least resistance within the framework; hence the exaggerated excuses stemming from a defensive attitude, which can lead only to further containment. Like the ballplayer of "Alibi Ike," Jack can come up with excuses that sound like boasts:

> Al: Well old pal what did I tell you about what I would do to that Boston Club? And now Al I have beat every club in the league this year because yesterday was the first time I beat the Boston Club this year but now I have beat all of them and most of them several times.
> This should ought to of gave me a record of 16 wins and 0 defeats because the only games I lost was throwed away behind me but instead of that my record is 10 games win and 6 defeats and that don't include the games I finished up and helped the other boys win which is about 6 more altogether but what do I care about my record Al? because I am not the kind of man that is always thinking about there record and playing for there record while I am satisfied if I give the club the best I got and if I win O.K. And if I lose who's fault is it. Not mine Al. (p. 158)

Truly, Jack Keefe stands out as a distorted personality because what he is can never measure up to what he would like to be. His busher code, in fact, is not the true code of the sporting hero, for, as Elder points out:

> in Ring's fiction baseball is an ordered world with definite rules of conduct; it demands skill and integrity and it has a code of honor. . . . Baseball implied an ethical ideal; and in Ring's work there is always an implied ethical ideal whether he is writing about sports or not. . . . His preoccupation with sport reflected a longing for an ideal world where the rules, if observed, guaranteed the triumph of merit; it also reflected his acute sense of the disparity between the way people were supposed to behave and the way they did. Sport provided Ring with a useful and significant scale for measuring his characters. Moreover the criteria of sport were especially valuable because everyone knew exactly what they were.[6]

[6]Elder, pp. 205-6.

In this "longing for an ideal world where the rules, if observed, guaranteed the triumph of merit," we recognize the credo of the sporting hero. It is also the motivation behind the art of Ring Lardner and the reason for the failure of a Jack Keefe. In Jack we have the embodiment of the person who cannot perceive the criteria or rules of the "ordered world" because he persists in always making his own set of rules. Thus the disparity between the world of sport and that of Jack Keefe affords Lardner an excellent opportunity to criticize the busher attitude.

In one main area of experience, however, Jack is more in keeping with the archetype of the sporting hero, that of his dealings with women. Near the beginning of his letters home Jack asserts that he is "going to leave the skirts alone," but this pledge is soon forgotten as he starts to fancy himself a "ladykiller." But his first love, Violet, deceives him. He writes:

> It is all off between Violet and I. She wasn't the sort of girl I suspected. She is just like them all Al. No heart. I wrote her a letter from Chicago telling her I was sold to San Francisco and she wrote back a postcard saying something about not haveing no time to waste on bushers. What do you know about that Al? Calling me a busher.[7]

Two months later Jack writes that he is engaged to a Hazel Carney, who is "some queen, Al—a great big stropping girl that must weigh one hundred and sixty lbs." In the meantime Violet attempts a reconciliation when Jack is reinstated with the White Sox, but he tells her he is engaged now. When he returns from a road trip, though, he discovers that Hazel has gone ahead and married a boxer. Now to Jack, Hazel is "no good and I was sorry the minute I agreed to marry her." Now he

[7]Lardner, p. 53.

believes himself free to marry Violet, who has "got Hazel beat forty ways." But Violet has other ideas. She marries a big lefthander, a species that Jack detests. He is now "through with girls," but a few days later writes Al that he is marrying Florence, a girl whom he meets through one of his teammates.

With his marriage to Florrie, Jack's real troubles begin. Stingier than ever, Jack, it seems, had not counted on the extra expense of a wife. His utterly tact-less ways with women help to estrange him even more:

> I and Florrie had our first quarrle the other night. I guess I told you the start of it but I don't remember. I made some crack about Violet and Hazel just to tease Florrie and she wanted to know who they was and I would not tell her. So she gets sore and goes over to Marie's [her sister] to stay all night. (p. 87)

After a series of domestic disputes in which Jack discov-ers what every married male learns sooner or later, that "they is not no use fusing with girls Al specially when they is your wife," Florrie packs up and leaves him. Once again he swears off women: "I am off of them all. They can all of them die and I should not worry." But he has obviously not forgotten their significance in his life, for when he pitches against Detroit he beans the pitcher who had stolen Violet from him, blowing the game and receiving a fine in the process. The birth of a son brings Jack and Florrie back together, but his petti-ness is evident more than ever since he is over-attentive to the baby, even accusing his wife of neglect. Jack's marriage, we feel, is doomed to perennial disruption simply because his private vision of life allows him to see things only his way.

In an overall view, *You Know Me Al* is primarily con-cerned with the lack of communication among individu-

als in an urban society. Jack Keefe's "encounter" with
the demands of society causes him to interpret them as
threats to the security and welfare of his being. His is
basically the fear of a Brom Bones, who must rid the
community of any threat to his established image.
Paradoxically, though, Jack never establishes an image;
consequently his attempt at self-definition—his quest for
money and inner security as well as his hope of getting
along with the girls—is doomed to failure, because he is
basically an innocent moving in an alien world. Perhaps
it is for this reason that Ring Lardner created such a
vivid portrait. Lardner himself was an alien in a cruel,
oftentimes unsympathetic world, and he knew well and
sympathized with the sort of person he was criticizing.

The Neon Wilderness and the Military Machine: Two Variations on a Theme

> In the heart of the city, in the heat of midsummer, the
> platform had sheltered him. Now he remembered the sun
> as a hostile thing coming between the El ties; remembered
> sunlight as others recall it seen through trees or climbing
> vines.
>
> —Nelson Algren, *Never Come Morning*

> "back in the time of the pioneers, a man could do what he
> wanted to do, in peace. But he had the woods then, he
> could go off in the woods and live alone. He could live well
> off the woods. And if they followed him there for this or
> that, he could just move on. There was always more woods
> on up ahead. But a man cant do that now. He's got to play
> ball with them."
>
> —James Jones, *From Here to Eternity*

Of all sports used by American writers to project and
criticize an impersonal way of life, boxing has been an
obvious choice, since it can so characteristically represent

the unscrupulous ways of a callous system. By extension, boxing in literature becomes symbolic of that way of life in which a man finds himself struggling against insurmountable odds. In varying degrees we find this predicament operative in works ranging from Lardner's "Champion" (1916) and Hemingway's "Fifty Grand" (1927) to Budd Schulberg's *The Harder They Fall* (1947), and more recently Leonard Gardner's brilliant *Fat City* (1969). Perhaps the prototype of all these stories is Jack London's "A Piece of Steak" (1912), certainly a representative story, because in it the villain, boxing, is directly equated with life.

Since London was primarily concerned with relating the Success Myth to the reality of life around it, we observe that there is something of the athletic manner about all his heroes. He may always sympathize with the underdog, but his heroes possess the competitive sense of the athlete; and as Kenneth Lynn has observed, all London's work is permeated by a "morality which measures all things in terms of effort and accomplishment."[8] But with London the sense of accomplishment is never equal to the expense of effort, for he always asserts that the potential greatness of the individual is nearly always crushed by superior forces. Consequently, for London the American Dream becomes a nightmare, and the controlling athletic metaphor of his stories is one in which the odds are set by an unbeatable system.

In "A Piece of Steak" the implication that the system of organized boxing is akin to life itself is evidence of London's conviction that one can never expect things to go his way when he would most like them to. Tom King, a veteran of many ring wars, would like to win one more fight and quit for the "missus and kiddies." Wise in ring

[8]Kenneth Lynn, *The Dream of Success: A Study of the Modern American Imagination* (Boston: Little, Brown & Co., 1955), p. 76.

savvy, King makes effective use of his great advantage of experience. Even so, the "system" must have its way, and after King has outpointed his younger opponent all the way, in the end he is knocked out by him. As King expresses his predicament: "Always were these youngsters rising up in the boxing game, springing through the ropes and shouting their defiance; and always were the old uns going down before them."[9] Sorry, but this is the way life is, suggests London. The dream of success can never be greater than the facts surrounding it. Even King's inability to get the piece of steak that he felt might have given him the strength to win is a portent of his eventual submission to overwhelming odds. King's function in this story, as it is with any dissociated London hero, is to show the difference between the real and ideal, a theme that has been taken up by many an American writer concerned with the disillusionment growing out of the facts of existence.

Two novels of modern America that treat this theme effectively are Nelson Algren's *Never Come Morning* (1942) and James Jones's *From Here to Eternity* (1951). In both novels the heroes are boxers, who can also be seen as variations of the traditional sporting hero in American literature. As indicated, boxing is almost always identified with the impersonal manner of a system or institution. In *Never Come Morning* boxing is used to reveal the bleakness and futility of Lefty Bicek's ghetto experiences; in *From Here to Eternity* this sport is drawn upon in such a way as to suggest Prewitt's subservient relationship to the Army, his real antagonist. As with all the heroes of this section, the experience of encounter of both Bicek and Prewitt grows out of their reaction to the society within which they find themselves. Although the pattern of encounter reminds Bicek and Prewitt that

[9]Jack London, "A Piece of Steak," from *Jack London's Tales of Adventure*, ed. Irving Shepard (Garden City, N.Y.: Hanover House, 1956), p. 417.

they possess the potential for a better life, it is the society itself that denies them this outcome in the end.

In the American naturalistic novel it is always the city or system itself that functions as antagonist, the cold, impersonal, structured society that creates what seem to be insuperable conditions within which the protagonist is doomed to struggle hopelessly. The struggle itself is indicative of the hero's desire for a better life, but the futility of the struggle is in itself a telling comment on modern man's subjugation to an urbanized society. The central irony of *Never Come Morning* is that Lefty Bicek, a product of the Polish slums of Chicago, dreams of escaping this world through his ability in a sport that is at once a creation of urbanized forces and a symbol of Lefty's struggle within the system. One critic has observed that

> Lefty is in quest of a more meaningful life than he sees available to him in the street, but he cannot escape the street, and what it offers becomes the ordering principle of his life. Because there is nothing else he dreams of glory in the ring or on the ball field, dreams which are substitutes for the boredom he endures or which are compensation for the lack of status which constantly humiliates him.[10]

Status achievement, or the inherent desire to be the best within one's self-created world of values, is another important characteristic of the traditional sporting hero and is Lefty's incentive for escaping his environment. But the image of the prison cell looms too large in *Never Come Morning,* and in a general sense the most inescapable cell of all is the city itself, the "neon wilderness" that subjugates, in contrast to Natty's or even Ike's "wilderness" that frees. Because the community has failed to give substance and meaning to Lefty's place in life, the

[10]Chester E. Eisinger, *Fiction of the Forties* (Chicago: University of Chicago Press, 1963), p. 79.

metaphor of the wilderness becomes perverted to the extent that Lefty feels hostile to those things that characterize the true wilderness:

> Reared in fear of cold and hunger, he retained a wistful longing for the warmth and security of the womb; there it was always warm. It felt like a half-memory in him when he came to any dark windless place; he could not recall a time when he had not preferred silence and darkness to daylight and struggle.[11]

For Lefty the sporting hero's quest has become inverted. In contrast to the image of Natty and Ike as successful hunters, Lefty visualizes himself as a hunter who never captures the spoils of the hunt:

> He had once seen a wolf's head in a Milwaukee Avenue taxidermist's window, above a bare varnished floor with nothing around but a couple chairs and empty paint can lying on its side. He had thought dimly of himself, since, as a hunter in a barren place. "I been hungry all my life, all the time," he told himself, "I never get my teeth into anythin' all my own." (p. 32)

Algren's recurrent references to the jungle of the city emphasize its overpowering presence in the novel and the fact that Lefty can never really avoid its grip on his destiny. Even when he takes his girl to an amusement park, the cold fact of the city's proximity is forced upon him as from his vantage point on the roller coaster he looks out on

> thousands of little people and hundreds of bright little stands, and over it all the coal-smoke pall of the river factories and railroad yards. He saw in that moment the whole dim-lit city on the last night of summer; the troubled streets that led to the abandoned beaches, the for-rent signs

[11]Nelson Algren, *Never Come Morning* (New York: Harper & Row Perennial Library, 1965), p. 31.

above hotels and furnished basement rooms, moving trol-
leys and rising bridges: the cagework city, beneath a coalsmoke sky. (p. 59)

The pervasive atmosphere of *Never Come Morning* is due
in large part to Algren's intent of always painting Lefty
Bicek's Chicago as a "cagework city, beneath a coalsmoke
sky," which may be in the best tradition of American
realism but at times borders on the surrealistic, for the
horror of Lefty's environment is really the landscape of
nightmare.

As it focuses itself through Lefty's experience, the isolation of his environment is dramatically revealed
through his time spent in jail after being picked up by
the police for having a part in the shooting of a drunk.
The essential misunderstanding that exists between of-
fenders in a society and those who enforce its laws is
brought out not only by Algren's reference to the sign in
the police station that reads

I HAVE ONLY
MYSELF TO BLAME
FOR MY FALL

but also through the feeling and atmosphere he manages to convey in the ensuing cell scenes:

> it was not until he raised his voice and the whole cell rang
> that he realized he was alone. That there was no one, above
> or below or near at hand, or down the corridor to hear.
> That no one was coming to see him, that no one was feel-
> ing badly about his being in here. (p. 84)

And later:

> When he lay down he felt he was in this cell for life. Felt
> walls and bars, for the first time, as walls and bars. . . . He
> knew at last where he was, and it did not seem to him that,

even though he were freed in the morning, that he would ever be free again. (p. 91)

Significantly, Lefty's type of "aloneness" offers a startling contrast to that of a Santiago, whose lonely quest ultimately frees rather than imprisons. In Lefty Bicek's mind, freedom from whatever would restrict him and his sense of status can be temporarily realized only through his dream of himself as either a sensational baseball pitcher or as the heavyweight champion of the world. Consequently, in his moments of personal crisis he resorts to this kind of reverie, dreaming of a world in which the cold, hard externalities of his existence instantly disappear, and dream and reality merge into the kind of world he longs to identify with.

A revealing factor defining the crisis in Lefty's life grows out of his estranged relationship with women, a predicament most clearly shown in his tortured love for Steffi, the girl friend he unwittingly sends headlong into a life of prostitution. As a type of the sporting hero, Lefty is fearful of the restrictions on one's personal identity that the good woman stands for:

> But what could you do with a girl once she was yours? You couldn't keep on just sleeping around, above a poolroom or on the beach or in a corner as though she were some Clark Street tramp. If you did you'd make a Clark Street tramp out of her. (pp. 34-35)

Lefty's attitude toward women is the result of a tension between his own private concept of what a woman should be and the demands of the group he is a part of, which sees the female's prime relationship with the male as nothing more than the satisfying of a biological urge. Observe his reaction when he is with Steffi at the amusement park: "The thought broke over him like another man's idea: 'Get some liquor in her. That's what dames are for'" (p. 55). As another variation of the sporting myth whose code of behavior is perverted by the demands of society, Lefty Bicek's actions clearly show him as a victim of group demands. The most significant event pointing this event out, of course, is his allowing the mass rape of Steffi by members of his athletic club, a criminal act the import of which could be interpreted symbolically or psychologically as deriving from the sporting mind's basic fear of woman and what she represents. But the impact of what Lefty has allowed to happen haunts him throughout the novel. Still, he rationalizes his actions as being in accord with the will of the group:

> According to his code he had done no more for Catfoot and the others than Catfoot and the others had at times done for him. He had been straight with the boys, he had been regular. . . .
> "A guy got to be practical about women," he comforted himself. And *hadn't* he been practical? He'd made her, hadn't he? He'd scored and so the other sports had scored—if that wasn't being straight he'd like to know what was." (p. 127)

Right from the beginning Lefty's relationship with Steffi is on a strained basis. After taking advantage of her in her mother's rooms above the poolroom, Lefty feels that he must "make it up to her." He takes her to the amusement park, but his uneasiness in her presence is accentuated by another one of his sports reveries while he is pitching balls to win a kewpie doll. In his thoughts he is no longer in an amusement park trying to win a doll for his girl; instead, "he was on the mound at Comiskey Park under a burning July sun with three and two on the batter and the sun in his eyes. . . ." He wins the doll for Steffi, but he rips the head off as if to destroy their intimacy, which has interrupted his dream of a world outside his present existence but one he yearns to identify with:

> To be a man out there in the world of men. To be against men, any other men, with a hard-fought game behind him and the hardest hitter in front of him and the trickiest runner behind him; pouring sweat, the breaks going against him, aching in his great left arm every time he raised it; but forever in there trying, not caring that they were all against him because they were making a man out of him by being against him. Pitching out his arm and his heart and his life. But in there pitching. To be a man in the world of men. (p. 52)

Expressed again is the recurring dream of the sporting hero in American fiction, that participation in the ritual of the competitive act will bring about improvement of performance and, by extension, self-image. From our earliest literature on, the sporting hero appears more at ease in his womanless world, and if women do enter the picture, it is only to complicate his existence, a situation equally as true for Ike McCaslin as it is for Lefty Bicek.

Thus the hard facts of Lefty's unfortunate life compel him to create an imaginary world in which he is champion and the most serious problem he has to face is ridding his world of the outsider's challenge, represented in his mind by the Jew and the Negro. After he is jailed for his part in a mugging, alone in his cell he imagines himself as the "new 195-pound white hope" fighting for the title:

> Bicek came out so fast at the bell that the Jew hadn't gotten his robe off—was standing there with one arm free and the other all caught up and the customers . . . urging Bicek to finish him off then and there. . . . This Bicek wasn't one to take advantage of man, woman, or child. Just a big, clean

kid, he'd be a clean champ, and he let the Jew clean free of
his robe now. Cheers. Hisses. Catcalls. Applause. Father
Francis blessed the boy openly from the third row. (p. 87)

In his own mind Lefty practices a code of fair play that
is just as meaningful as Natty Bumppo's, but as another
product of urban environment his vision is blurred,
since a great part of his code is based on his own private
prejudices, views that spring from his fear that what little status he does have will be undermined by an outsider.

The powerful conclusion of the novel, though, is that
Lefty can have neither status nor security. He can only
dream about these things that are denied him in the
"neon wilderness." Many times this sense of frustration
is expressed through the imagery of the fight game itself. Observe Lefty's feeling about his relationship with
the law, that it was as though "he were in a ring with an
opponent he couldn't see." Such an image conveys precisely the predicament of Lefty Bicek as sporting hero,
for like many modern fictional heroes, Lefty's great flaw
is one of vision, and Algren's use of the night as Lefty's
natural environment is a brilliant stroke that further
emphasizes his inability to "see." Truly Lefty Bicek's
world is one in which night is eternal and morning
never comes. It is a world in which the formula in the
Jack London story holds true, for even though Lefty
wins his big fight at the end of the novel and a reconciliation with Steffi seems in the offing, the law, his old
enemy, catches up with him again and he is booked on a
murder charge. The pattern of encounter in *Never Come
Morning* manifests itself through the experience of Lefty
Bicek in such a way that we are repeatedly reminded of
the wide gulf separating dream and fact in American
life.

Robert E. Lee Prewitt, the "bolshevik" protagonist of James Jones's *From Here to Eternity,* presents a fascinating study in the meaning of individualism in the modern world. Like Lefty Bicek, Prewitt is a displaced person searching for identity in a system whose chief end is to remind the individual that he has no identity. Or at least, as we recognize it, the efficiency of any military organization is based on its power to mold the individual will to the purpose of the group. But Prewitt, in order to retain his own personal sense of self, rebels against the restrictions that the organization imposes upon him. When we first meet Prewitt he is transferring into a new outfit. He has quit his former Company's boxing team after having blinded an opponent in the ring. Because those who control the sport will not let him alone in their efforts to get him back in the ring, Prewitt requests transfer in order to follow his own mind, or at least he deceives himself into thinking that he might be able to. Prewitt's respect for the worth of the individual is contained in his attitude toward boxing:

> the whole thing of ring fighting was hurting somebody else, deliberately, and particularly when it was not necessary. Two men who have nothing against each other get in a ring and try to hurt each other, to provide vicarious fear for people with less guts than themselves. And to cover it up they called it sport and gambled on it.[12]

But the Company Commander of his new outfit turns out to be a "jockstrap" who wants to win the Regimental championships to improve his chance for rank; therefore he would impress Prewitt back into the ring. The feeling, then, is that Prewitt should seriously consider representing his new Company in the ring, for as Maggio, his spiritual brother, reminds him when they first

[12]James Jones, *From Here to Eternity* (New York: New American Library Signet Books, 1964), p. 27.

meet, there is one sure way of getting along in G Company: "If you're smart you'll learn to jockstrap, and learn quick, and get on the gravytrain, if you want to be a successful soljer" (p. 43).

Even though Prewitt's first meeting with Capt. Holmes is one in which the CO indicates that they will not try to pressure him into fighting against his will, it is evident what Holmes's intentions really are. He tells Prewitt:

> "you should know that in the Army its not the individual that counts. Every man has certain responsibilities to fulfill. Moral responsibilities that go beyond the ARs' regulations. It might look as though I were a free agent, but I'm not. No matter how high you get there is always somebody over you, and who knows more about it all than you do." (p. 50)

This, of course, is the way the military operates, but in a larger sense society functions in this manner also. Col. Delbert, the Regiment's Commander and naturally higher in the system than Holmes, tells him:

> "Your company interests me. It proves my theory: good athletes make good noncoms and good leaders; good leaders make a good organization. Simple logic. Plenty of cattle in the world, that have to be driven. But without good leaders nothing's ever accomplished." (p. 59)

But to Prewitt's way of thinking, to seek out a personal identity does not mean to bend to the Army's definition of what a leader is. Nor does he look upon himself as among the "cattle" of the world. The penalty for Prewitt's outlook is a state of dissociation brought on by a refusal to identify with any particular side. As a result, his sense of isolation is heightened to the point that he can refer to his arrival in the new Company as follows: "It was always unpleasant, moving like this; it always brought home to you the essential rootlessness of yourself and all men like you, always on the move, never really stopping anywhere, never really home" (p. 70). The instinctive mobility of the sporting hero becomes for Prewitt a passive act that compels him to encounter continually the enigma of his own self, never arriving at any sure sense of identity. Prewitt's type of mobility starkly contrasts with that of Hemingway's Nick Adams, who, having been a part of the military, has his "river" to retreat to. Yet, the paradox of the passive athlete is essential in getting across Jones's message: the performer who will not play ball according to the rules becomes a victim of the contest or, in this case, system, which is precisely what happens to Prewitt.

Prewitt's belief that "every man has certain rights" is contested by Stark, the Mess Sergeant. He tells Prewitt:

> "you're going on the idea of the world as people say it is, instead of as it really is. In this world, no man really has any rights at all. Except what rights he can grab holt of and hang on to. And usually the only way he can get *them* is by taking them away from someone else." (p. 206)

Stark is right about Prewitt's outlook being compounded of illusion, for primarily Prewitt's problems arise from an idealism that does not match the facts of existence. The U.S. Army as a symbol of the world "as it really is" is a vast system that demands certain key responses on different levels if the machine is to function efficiently. Prewitt's tragedy, then, is that in such a system he would dare to follow a code based on his idea of the system as he would like it to be.

Like his brothers of the sporting code, Prewitt rejects the demands of a society to placate his own sense of integrity. Again we observe the anti-feminine attitude in which the woman, whether prostitute or prude, represents social restrictions that are alien to a life like

Prewitt's. A woman is good only insofar as she aids in projecting the male ego, usually accomplished—or in many cases defeated—through the sexual encounter. In such naturalistic writing describing the intimate relations of men and women there is a "barely veiled hatred and fear of women, who are so essential to men and so delicious, but whose sexuality is designed to subdue and tame (and destroy) the masculine integrity, the masculine virility."[13] The essential estrangement that exists between Prewitt and his women is graphically brought out in his relationship with Violet, his highly prized "shack-job":

> As he moved over her, he realized again that he did not know her face or name, that here in this act that brings two human fantasies as close as they can ever come, so close that one moves inside the other, he still did not know her, nor she him, nor could they touch each other. To a man who lives his life among the flat hairy angularities of other men, all women are round and soft, and all are inscrutable and strange.[14]

In the world of Prewitt love and marriage are impossible, since both represent entrapment, an inherent fear of the individual who has expressed himself in sporting endeavor. Or as Prewitt expresses it: "A guy like me aint got no business bein married. I'm a soljer." Only Prewitt would be a soldier on his own terms. In Lorene, the prostitute, he thinks he has found a real woman, one he would even like to marry, but later he discovers that she, too, represents a threat to his private world and that his love for her is nothing more than illusion. Everything else has become illusion, too, and after his AWOL period with Lorene (Alma), he reasons that the life of

[13]Maxwell Geismar, *American Moderns: From Rebellion to Conformity* (New York: Hill and Wang, 1958), pp. 232-33.
[14]Jones, pp. 91-92.

the thirty-year-man is the only reality for him. But shortly after the Japanese have attacked Pearl Harbor, Prewitt, on his way back to join the Company, is shot and killed by a patrol.

As in *Never Come Morning*, imagery of confinement appears throughout *From Here to Eternity*, the major significance of which appears in the section dealing with Prewitt's experiences in the stockade. When he is first put under arrest, Prewitt reflects:

> he knew all about jails jails were just as intimate to his life and heritage as being on the bum or soldiering . . . he had learned jails even before he learned the Army in fact they kind of seemed to go together. (p. 488)

As Jones presents it, all of Prewitt's life has been an impossible attempt to escape confinement. He had joined the Army to get away from the bleak life of the Kentucky mountain region. In the Army he has sought to express himself both as a boxer and a bugler, but a venereal infection fouls up his record (his initial experience with woman as enemy), and he is transferred to Hawaii's Schofield Barracks, where the main action of the story takes place. Here, Prewitt's refusal to fight at the behest of Capt. Holmes or anyone else creates a series of situations that eventually result in his imprisonment in the stockade.

Conformity itself represents a kind of imprisonment, we recognize, but in Prewitt's case we also realize that the price one pays to maintain a sense of individuality is confinement within the cell of the self. Thus the stockade and all its nightmarish atmosphere become symbolic of this peculiar kind of imprisonment. Instead of molding Prewitt to the system, though, his sentence of confinement only serves to distort his special kind of identity, driving him further into the prison of self. Practicing an athletic asceticism to endure the horrors of the stockade, Prewitt develops a philosophy of pain and passive resistance that prepares him for the final estrangement from the way of life which would deny him his personal expression. After witnessing the sadistic brutality of Sgt. Judson on inmates of the Stockade, Prewitt decides that when he gets out, he will track Judson down and kill him, if only for the reason that this act will make him a man again. To kill Fatso Judson is to kill the system, but paradoxically, in doing so Prewitt further isolates himself. He goes AWOL, realizes the futility of his relationship with Lorene, and is finally killed in a tragic mishap. In death his estrangement is complete.

Prewitt, then, is among the most tragic of the sporting heroes. His tragedy is compounded of the fact that, like all heroes of the sporting myth, he is compelled to face the realities of the self and choose a code of action that either frees or delimits his inner being. Characteristically, Prewitt decides on a code of self-definition that cannot be realized in an organization that discourages such expression. His predicament is that of many areas of modern experience, in which the meaning of survival is dependent upon the degree to which one is willing to sacrifice his identity. But with Prewitt there can be no compromise in the encounter, and because of such an attitude his life moves inevitably toward its tragic conclusion. It is pertinent to note that one of the few persons of the "system" that Prewitt respects, M/Sgt. Warden, abides by a Hemingway-like code that Prewitt greatly admires:

> it was . . . as if The Warden had applied to his whole life the principle which applied to all other games of sport—that laying down of certain arbitrary rules to make success that much harder for the player to attain, like clipping in foot-

ball or traveling in basketball, or in the same way, as he had
read someplace, that sporting fishermen would use the
light six-nine tackle in fishing for sailfish instead of the
heavy tackle that makes it easy for the novice, thereby im-
posing upon themselves voluntarily the harder conditions
that make the reward worth more to them. (p. 270)

Like Hemingway's old fisherman, Prewitt would wel-
come the "harder conditions," not only because they
make the "reward worth more" but because through
them one can realize identity and foster greater respect
for the worth of the individual.

The Message of Satire: The Ex-College Athlete and the Groping for Maturity

the ability to "play the game" has a greater appeal to the
American imagination than intellectual or artistic accom-
plishment.
—Cozens and Stumpf, *Sports in American Life*

The fact that in America the majority of ex-college
athletes carry their innate competitive sense on into the
world of big business helps make the businessman a
grand object for satire in American fiction. Since satire
is focused on the distance between what really is and
what is not, the ex-college football hero, for example, is
almost always a choice selection to show this disparity. It
is the ex-athlete, who, ironically in many cases, continues
to disregard the realities of life in order to make the
business of living into a kind of game with rules based
on his individual interpretation of how the game should
be played. We see this businessman-athlete type recurring in the works of Sinclair Lewis and John O'Hara as
well as in many authors of lesser note—the kind of
character who answers Van Wyck Brooks's description

that the American businessman is a "child-like being, moved and movable, the player of a game, a sportsman essentially, though with a frequently dim perception of the rules."[15] This last phrase aptly applies to the athlete turned businessman, because when he is presented for satirical purposes his personal failure is essentially one of vision and his inability to distinguish values during the encounter experience. Like a child, he cannot see himself clearly in relationship to his environment, and in this so-called innocent state is compelled to relate everything to his own ego-centered world. The result is lack of self-awareness and a failure in communication, not only in marriage but in social dealings as well. The only real world for him is, and always will be, we recognize, the world of the game. As early as F. Scott Fitzgerald's portrait of Tom Buchanan in *The Great Gatsby* (1925), we are given an important clue to the reason for such an outlook. Tom as an All-American football player at Yale is described as "one of those men who reach such an acute limited excellence at twenty-one that everything afterward savors of anticlimax."[16] For the star athlete nothing in life can ever again approach the significance of the lost world of the Big Game. Consequently, the experience of encounter for characters like these cannot be realized in life, but only in a game or contest.

In many instances it is the "most-likely-to-succeed" person who comes in for criticism, of which a noteworthy figure is J. P. Marquand's Bo-Jo Brown. In his preface to *H. M. Pulham, Esq.* (1941), Marquand says that Bo-Jo, a Harvard graduate, "is intended to be recognized at once as a familiar type formed by college athletics." And so he is. We all recognize the joke-telling,

[15]Van Wyck Brooks, *America's Coming-of-Age* (New York: E. P. Dutton & Co., 1958), p. 69.

[16]F. Scott Fitzgerald, *The Great Gatsby* (New York: Charles Scribner's Sons, 1953), p. 6.

alumni-leading, and project-engineering personality that Bo-Jo is. (For the twenty-fifth reunion of his class, Bo-Jo proposes a professional boxing bout to be staged in Harvard Yard!) Such individuals, we feel, are harmless, but woefully superficial—a far cry from the agonizing Ray Blent of Howard Nemerov's *The Homecoming Game* (1957). But Blent offers to throw a game for money, something that would never have entered Bo-Jo Brown's thoughts. Nemerov, though, is primarily satirizing the system of college football, not so much individuals, an intent we realize on one occasion when his professor-hero reflects:

> I enjoy football games. Fine, clean American sport, best amateur tradition, lots of color, great for building character, gets everyone out in the fresh air once a week. That's all splendid. The fine young men who play it are largely hired men, but they are not paid enough to be called professionals. The game presents an image of war; it has a symbolic meaning, a value of the sort, and now and then someone breaks his neck at it, so it also has an element of reality.[17]

The game of football might have an "element of reality" about it, but it has obviously never rubbed off on characters like Bo-Jo Brown, at least insofar as the game's realistic elements can be applied to life, for, as it has been observed, "the unimaginative, the former football heroes like Bo-Jo Brown, may accommodate themselves so completely to encumbrances that they are hardly aware of their predicament."[18] The complexities of modern society make self-knowledge an impossible task for such people, but even sporting characters used for satirical purposes show evidence, though in a dis-

[17]Howard Nemerov, *The Homecoming Game* (New York: Simon and Schuster, 1957), p. 121.
[18]John J. Gross, *John P. Marquand* (New York: Twayne, 1963), p. 66.

torted sense, of the traditional sporting hero's innocent background.

A highly outstanding example of this kind of character is presented in Philip Roth's *Goodbye, Columbus* (1959) in Ron Patimkin, whom Alfred Kazin calls "the thickest, dumbest, solidest, most amiable American football hero yet."[19] Actually, Ron's sport is basketball, but choice of sport is of little consequence here. Observe, also, that Ron's Jewish heritage has little to do with his role of seeking meaningful identity, since both his wealth and athletic ability have entrenched him as an "insider," in contrast to the uncertain but more perceptive narrator of the story, Neil Klugman. In respect to the Jew's position in American fiction as moving from marginal figure to one of centrality, Harvey Swados has some interesting comments concerning Ron Patimkin:

> We might measure the distance that has been traveled by contrasting Hemingway's Jewish athlete of the Twenties, Robert Cohn, the boxer, forever attempting with fists and flattery to join the club, the expatriate Americans who exclude him, to Philip Roth's Jewish athlete of the Fifties, Ronald Patimkin, who hangs his jockstrap from the shower faucet while he sings the latest pop tunes, and is so completely the self-satisfied muscle-bound numskull that notions of Jewish alienation are entirely "foreign" to him.[20]

Ron is a recent graduate of Ohio State University, where he played varsity basketball, which is apparently about all the education he needs to work his way up in his father's business, Patimkin Kitchen and Bathroom Sinks. At the farthest extreme from an Ike McCaslin, Ron, another "innocent," will of course remain impervious to the implication of any misfortune that might chance his

[19]Alfred Kazin, *Contemporaries* (Boston: Atlantic-Little, Brown & Co., 1962), p. 174.

[20]Harvey Swados, *A Radical's America* (Boston: Little, Brown & Co., 1962), p. 174.

way, if any actually should. When his wedding is announced, Ron's sister, Brenda, feels that now he will have "responsibilities":

> And at dinner Ron expanded on the subject of responsibilities and the future.
> "We're going to have a boy," he said, to his mother's delight, "and when he's about six months old I'm going to sit him down with a basketball in front of him, and a football, and a baseball, and then whichever one he reaches for, that's the one we're going to concentrate on."[21]

To Ron, "responsibilities" are all resolved in the world of the game, for there can be no problem comparable to being down by ten points with two minutes to play. Since Ron Patimkin persists in living in a vacuous and artificial imitation of life (he identifies with the saccharine music of Mantovani and André Kostelanetz), his life style is far from the concept of the true hero as one who learns to see things as they are through his struggles, thereby arriving at a degree of self-knowledge.

The ironic title, *Goodbye, Columbus,* refers to the fact that Ron Patimkin has never left the campus at Columbus, Ohio, and like most ex-athletes of his stripe probably never will. He is fond of playing what he calls his "Columbus record," a recording of the school year's events in nostalgic retrospect given to all the graduating seniors. In it he hears a "Voice, bowel-deep and historic," reminiscing of his last year at the University —Fraternity Row in the golden glow of autumn, the big football game with Illinois, and finally the basketball game that is the last one for seniors:

> "And here comes Ron Patimkin dribbling out. Ron, Number 11, from Short Hills, New Jersey. Big Ron's last

[21]Philip Roth, *Goodbye, Columbus* (New York: Bantam Books, 1963), p. 6.

game, and it'll be some time before Buckeye fans forget
him. . . ."

Big Ron tightened on his bed as the loudspeaker called
his name; his ovation must have set the nets to trembling.

Finally, commencement arrives, and the Voice continues:

"For many this will be the last glimpse of the campus, of
Columbus, for many years. Life calls us, and anxiously if
not nervously we walk out into the world and away from
the pleasures of these ivied walls. But not from its
memories. . . ."
There was goose flesh in Ron's veiny arms as the Voice
continued. "We offer ourselves to you then, world, and
come at you in search of Life. And to you, Ohio State, to
you Columbus, we say thank you, thank you and goodbye.
We will miss you, in the fall, in the spring, but someday we
shall return. Till then, goodbye, Ohio State, goodbye, red
and white, goodbye Columbus . . . goodbye, Columbus
. . . goodbye." (pp. 74-75)

"Life" with a capital "L" is Ron Patimkin's special brand
of existence—an artificial, commencement-speech kind
of life, inspired by memories of the past and the un-
realistic clichés of how "the game" should be played, typical of which is the dictum asserting that to achieve a
goal one must play the game hard. As for Ron's father,
a self-made man, such a cliché applies to his real-life
success, and he is outwardly perturbed at his discovery
that Ron has had four years of college and "can't unload
a truck." But underneath, the elder Patimkin is hardly
concerned, for the son's shortcomings at work only emphasize the father's accomplishments. Mr. Patimkin tells
Neil, who believes himself in love with his daughter:

"A man works hard he's got something. You don't get anywhere sitting on your behind, you know. . . . The biggest

men in the country worked hard, believe me. Even Rocke-
feller. Success don't come easy."

And Neil reflects:

> I had the feeling that what had tempted him into this bar-
> rage of universals was probably the combination of Ron's
> performance and my presence—me, the outsider who
> might one day be an insider. . . .
> Mr. Patimkin looked out at Ron again. "Look at him, if
> he played basketball like that they'd throw him the hell off
> the court." But he was smiling when he said it. (pp. 66-67)

Ron Patimkin, as a satirical offshoot of the sporting
archetype in American fiction, is both blessed and
cursed by his own innocence. While feelings of self-
doubt and states of soul-searching will scarcely plague
him in his present situation, at the same time he will
never really see himself in the light of his true environment. Unlike his literary cousins of sporting background, the fact that Ron marries a woman "singularly
unconscious of a motive in others or herself" and who
seems "a perfect match" for him is another irony of his
predicament as sporting type that aids the story's satirical function. But even though Ron's story is subordinate
to that of Neil and Brenda, it is integral to the overall
meaning of *Goodbye, Columbus* in that it reinforces and
gives added significance to Neil's involvement with the
Patimkin family—Neil, who as the story's real "alien"
comes to the awareness that what he had thought was a
relationship of true love has merely been one of meaningless infatuation. The contrast of Neil's humble background with the *nouveau riche* attitudes of Ron and his
family may serve to underscore his position as outsider,
but it also substantiates the fact that in modern literature
the first step toward self-discovery is through doubt and

questioning, an experience that Ron Patimkin, secure in his self-esteem, will never have to endure.

   Although Christian Darling of Irwin Shaw's "The Eighty-Yard Run" (1941) strikes the reader as possessing somewhat more self-awareness than Ron Patimkin, they stand as spiritual brothers, with Darling, the older of the two, exemplifying what can happen after the fall from innocence. Even though Darling may lack the emotional maturity to face the problems of everyday living, he is aware of his situation in a way that Ron Patimkin could never be of his own. Returning to the college scene of what he believes to be the "high point" of his life—an eighty-yard run for a touchdown—Darling is moved to reflect on the difference between his present life and that of fifteen years ago, the contrast between his shattered marriage and the "high point"

> on an autumn afternoon, twenty years old and far from death, with the air coming easily into his lungs, and a deep feeling inside him that he could do anything, knock over anybody, outrun whatever had to be outrun.[22]

The eighty-yard run—even though, oddly enough, it was accomplished in practice and not in a game—recalls a finer hour for Christian Darling, a time that "for the first time in his life was not a meaningless confusion of men, sounds, speed" (p. 2). And as one recalls the memorable events of youthful innocence through sensory experience, so Shaw emphasizes this area of Darling's memory in order to heighten the contrast between a period of time that once seemed beautiful and

[22]Irwin Shaw, *Selected Short Stories* (New York: Modern Library, 1961), p. 16.

one that now appears distasteful. To carry out this intent Shaw describes Darling's feelings after his run in a highly sensory manner:

> The sweat poured off his face and soaked his jersey and he liked the feeling, the warm moistness lubricating his skin like oil. Off in a corner of the field some players were punting and the smack of leather against the ball came pleasantly through the afternoon air.

And afterwards in the shower there were

> the hot water steaming off his skin and the deep soapsuds and all the young voices singing with the water streaming down and towels going and managers running in and out and the sharp sweet smell of oil of wintergreen and everybody clapping him on the back as he dressed.

Then one of the managers looks after him by "wiping a cut on his leg with alcohol and iodine, the little sting making him realize suddenly how fresh and whole and solid his body felt." And finally, when he is finishing dressing, there are

> the softness of his shirt and the soft warmth of his wool socks and his flannel trousers a reward against his skin after the harsh pressure of the shoulder harness and thigh and hip pads. He drank three glasses of cold water, the liquid reaching down coldly inside of him, soothing the harsh dry places in his throat and belly left by the sweat and running and shouting of practice. (p. 3)

This is the kind of writing—summoning the general feeling of well-being and the youthful awareness of being alive, perhaps forever—that lends especial sharpness to the image of Darling as sporting hero.

At this time, though, the main thing that stands out in

Darling's mind is the ideal relationship, at least from his point of view, with his girl, Louise, who

> watched him faithfully in the games . . . and drove him around in her car keeping the top down because she was proud of him and wanted to show everybody she was Christian Darling's girl. She bought him crazy presents because her father was rich, watches, pipes, humidors, an icebox for beer for his room, curtains, wallets, a fifty-dollar dictionary. (p. 5)

However, it is an unnatural relationship, one designed to feed his own ego and childish vanity, and even after they are married and living in New York he continues to have meaningless affairs with other women. Thus Darling's reaction to the feminine principle stands as yet another version of the sporting hero's inability to comprehend the mysteries of woman.

When Louise's father's business fails after the stock market crash, they are forced to provide for themselves for the first time, with the inevitable result that Darling, compelled to see himself in a new and different light, discovers himself totally estranged from Louise. He takes to drink while Louise takes to new friends—an arty, sophisticated set who seem to know all the right things to talk about. The fact of his alienation from this group and the city life they represent dawns on Darling when he observes one of Louise's new, smart hats, and sees it as a symbol of

> big city, smart and knowing women drinking and dining with men other than their husbands, conversation about things a normal man wouldn't know much about, Frenchmen who painted as though they used their elbows instead of brushes, composers who wrote whole symphonies without a single melody in them, writers who knew all about politics and women who knew all about writers, the movement of the proletariat, Marx, somehow mixed up

> with five-dollar dinners and the best-looking women in America and fairies who made them laugh and half-sentences immediately understood and secretly hilarious and wives who called their husbands "Baby." (p. 10)

In vivid contrast with the masculine innocence of the playing field, the sophistication of the city is feminine in nature and therefore unfathomable to Darling, who is even unable to understand Louise's way of walking "along the streets of the city, excited, at home, soaking in all the million tides of New York without fear, with constant wonder" (p. 11). In the ensuing downhill years they had fought only once, and when they did she had "apologized as she might to a child." To Louise, obviously, Darling is still a boy.

Finally, even though he is thirty-five years old, it is Darling's youthful appearance ("broad shoulders and well-kept waist . . . carefully brushed hair and his honest, wrinkle-less face") that lands him a job as a tailor's representative traveling from college to college. It is this job that sets the stage for his return to the University and the site of his life's "high point." Here the failure of his life stands out in the light of the fact that he can never return to the beautiful life of his past, and Shaw concludes:

> He had practiced the wrong thing, perhaps. He hadn't practiced for 1929 and New York City and a girl who would turn into a woman. Somewhere, he thought, there must have been a point where she moved up to me, was even with me a moment, when I could have held her hand, if I'd known, held tight, gone with her. Well, he'd never known. Here he was on a playing field that was fifteen years away and his wife was in another city having dinner with another and better man, speaking with him a different, new language, a language nobody had ever taught him. (p. 16)

The closing pathetic scene of this neatly structured story, depicting a middle-aged man attempting to recapture what he thinks is the zenith of his life, reminds us that Darling, through the act of reliving his great run, may be in quest of rebirth, but

> it was only after he had sped over the goal line and slowed to a trot that he saw the boy and girl sitting together on the turf, looking at him wonderingly.
> He stopped short, dropping his arms. "I . . ." he said, gasping a little, though his condition was fine and the run hadn't winded him. "I—once I played here." (p. 17)

The reality of the present overshadows the past and condemns it as mere nostalgia; thus, in respect to Darling's special attitude toward his past and his experience since that time, rebirth is an impossibility, and he must continue to live within the prison of his own immaturity.

4

The Neo-Romantic Encounter

Introduction

If by the term *romantic* we mean to imply the state of being or condition that emphasizes individual achievement and freedom of personal expression, then the term *neo-romantic,* at least for the purpose of this study, is a necessary one to apply to those fictional heroes of contemporary literature who, like their antecedents, are romantics at heart, but because of the kind of world in which they find themselves are denied the freedom to express themselves naturally in the truly romantic sense of individual achievement.

Pervading "The Eighty-Yard Run" is this kind of neo-romantic sensibility that controls the meaning and atmosphere of much contemporary fiction. Christian Darling has a deep yearning for his past and a more meaningful life, but his symbolic "run" at the end of the story suggests his sense of loss and frustration as to how he may retrieve his lost world.

The neo-romantic hero, then, is a character who inherently knows what he wants in life—usually personal identity and a sense of achievement, but his inability to perceive or evaluate the significance of his actions frustrates his every move to regain his former, idyllic state. Even the domain of the game and the "great, good place" of the forest (nature) no longer hold the meaning they once did; in fact, in most cases they are no longer available to him.

Most neo-romantic types of the sporting myth appear as has-beens. Divorced from their former athletic identities, they endure a kind of death in life. But an interesting variation of this figure is that of the athlete who dies young, in that through dying in his prime he retains his state of innocence and contributes identity and significance to the character he is inevitably paired with. Significantly, it is the death of the character who lacks self-awareness that results in his spiritual brother's becoming self-knowledgeable. The paradox of the athletic figure as dying athlete or anti-hero is exemplary of the tendency in recent fiction to move from mythic toward ironic modes of expression. But, as Northrop Frye has pointed out, controlled use of irony can also suggest mythic dimensions, as we shall see in certain of the following representative examples of the neo-romantic sensibility.

Both John Knowles in *A Separate Peace* and Mark Harris in *Bang the Drum Slowly* make use of the dying-athlete theme to stress the worth of the personal identity. In both works, the relationship of two major characters is played off in such a way that the pattern of encounter projects a growth in self-knowledge for one of the major characters. In both works, too, the paradox of the athlete's dying young reinforces the meaning. The tone of these novels is neo-romantic in that the major characters are concerned either with recovering a more natural relationship with their environments or with arriving at a surer sense of identity.

Further evidence of the neo-romantic attitude is

found in the character of Cash Bentley, through whom John Cheever presents the problem of the has-been or aging athlete in his short story "O Youth and Beauty!" However, Cheever's sure sense of irony holds this story together, so that Cash's apparently successful outer appearance is sacrificed to the image of the champion track star he longs to retain, with the pathetic result that Cash's life becomes a travesty of his former athletic identity.

In *Rabbit, Run* John Updike's Rabbit Angstrom is a younger version of Cash Bentley. He, too, longs for the meaningful experience of his athletic past, but his passive approach to the realistic demands of life labels him a failure. His worship of self is almost religious in its intensity, but in the case of Rabbit as neo-romantic, we shall see that the traditional image of the sporting hero and his intimate relationship with nature has become inverted. Without ever relishing the sweat and pain of the pursuit, the urban hero's quality of mobility is an agonizing experience.

Perhaps the supreme achievement of the neo-romantic encounter is *The Natural,* in which Bernard Malamud relates the experience of his super-athlete, Roy Hobbs, to the mystical aspects of baseball in order to present the dominant themes of modern literature—the quest for identity, the breakdown in communication, and the failure of love. In Malamud's version of the sporting myth the American Dream can never be realized, but the suffering one undergoes in its pursuit can result in self-knowledge, a far greater accomplishment in Malamud's vision than material gain or fame.

The Death of Innocence: The Paradox of the Dying Athlete

it seemed clear that wars were not made by generations and

their special stupidities, but that wars were made instead by
something ignorant in the human heart.
                              —John Knowles, *A Separate Peace*

Dying old is in the cards, and you figure on it, and it happens to everybody, and you are willing to swallow it but
why should it happen young to Bruce?
                              —Mark Harris, *Bang the Drum Slowly*

The aura of innocence surrounding the traditional
figure of the sporting myth is compellingly dramatized
through the image of the dying athlete in both John
Knowles's *A Separate Peace* (1959) and Mark Harris's
Bang the Drum Slowly (1956). The predicament of dying
young when contrasted with the sporting hero's quest
for immortality is strikingly used in these novels to
comment on the meaning of individuality in our day. In
both works this definition grows out of the interrelationship of their two main characters—that between Gene
and Phineas in *A Separate Peace* and Henry Wiggen and
Bruce Pearson in *Bang the Drum Slowly*. In both novels,
too, the death of one character results in self-knowledge
for the other, who in both cases happens to be the narrator. While Gene Forrester gains a fuller understanding
of the evil that separates man from man, Henry Wiggen
acquires a greater respect for the worth and dignity of
the individual.

Essential encounter in *A Separate Peace,* while set
against the larger background of World War II, focuses
on the minor wars declared among the schoolboys of
Devon, a prominent New England preparatory school,
in order to explain the larger question of why wars
come about. The friendship between Gene and Phineas,
two offsetting personalities in that the former is a
superior student and the latter an accomplished athlete,
is eventually disrupted by what at first appears to be a

trifling incident but is later expanded to support the novel's inherent theme: wars are caused by "something ignorant in the human heart."

In schoolboy literature related to the sporting myth, the major conflict exists between the ivory tower and the playing field, or authority and self-expression; thus much of the significance of *A Separate Peace* is projected through the imagery and metaphor of the game. It is appropriate to observe here, too, that because they provide opportunity for self-expression, the playing fields of Devon are equated with the traditional wilderness of the sporting myth. As Gene informs us near the beginning of the novel:

> Beyond the gym and the fields began the woods, our, the Devon School's woods, which in my imagination were the beginning of the great northern forests. I thought that, from the Devon Woods, trees reached in an unbroken, widening corridor so far to the north that no one had ever seen the other end, somewhere up in the far unorganized tips of Canada. We seemed to be playing on the tame fringe of the last and greatest wilderness. I never found out whether this is so and perhaps it is.[1]

The playing field as representative of the forest in microcosm becomes the great, good place, or the "last and greatest wilderness," where the inherent innocence of Phineas can find true expression. As Gene sees it, Finny believed that

> "you always win at sports." This "you" was collective. Everyone always won at sports. . . . Finny never permitted himself to realize that when you won they lost. That would have destroyed the perfect beauty which was sport. Nothing bad ever happened in sports; they were the absolute good. (pp. 26-27)

[1]John Knowles, *A Separate Peace* (New York: Bantam Books, 1966), p. 23.

The game of blitzball, which Finny himself invents to perk up a dull summer at Devon, is more than an example of his ingratiating manner with his fellow students; the game is a symbol of his very being:

> He had unconsciously invented a game which brought his own athletic gifts to their highest pitch. The odds were tremendously against the ball carrier, so that Phineas was driven to exceed himself practically everyday when he carried the ball. To escape the wolf pack which all the other players became he created reverses and deceptions and acts of sheer mass hypnotism which were so extraordinary that they surprised even him; after some of these plays I would notice him chuckling quietly to himself, in a kind of happy disbelief. (p. 31)

Phineas has a Hemingwaylike devotion to enjoyment of sporting endeavor as a thing in itself. His breaking a school swimming record and not reporting his feat for the record emphasize both his uniqueness as an individual and his role as a type of the sporting hero, in that to Phineas the pursuit is more important than the goal. But his athletic accomplishments also add to the fear already present in the inner being of Gene, his roommate, and his best friend. Gene tells himself: "You and Phineas . . . are even in enmity. You are both coldly driving ahead for yourselves alone" (p. 45). But the interrelationship of both characters is structured to bring about the novel's tragic denouement and dramatize its basic theme.

As the story develops, Gene's gnawing but unfounded fear that Phineas, out of envy, is seeking to destroy his reputation as a student causes him to mistake Phineas's real intentions. The upshot of this is a betrayal by Gene that results eventually in the death of Phineas but ultimately in the self-education of Gene. The Super Suicide Society of the Summer Session is another one of Finny's improvisations that not only brings out his athletic ability but also further endears himself to his adventure-starved classmates. To become a member of this "secret" organization one must merely leap from a tree limb that hangs treacherously over the river skirting the Devon campus. But Finny, ever the daredevil, proposes that he and Gene jump together. Gene, for some unaccountable reason, which he later explains to Phineas as "just some ignorance inside me, some crazy thing inside me, something blind," jounces the limb, causing Finny to fall to earth and break a leg. Still the innocent, Phineas, even though now physically through with sports, vicariously continues to identify with the sporting encounter through Gene: "Listen, pal, if *I* can't play sports, you're going to play them for me." To which command Gene feels that "I lost part of myself to him then . . . this must have been my purpose from the first: to become a part of Phineas" (p. 77).

If, like many another figure in American literature, Phineas becomes a victim of his own innocence, then Gene, through his confrontation with the force of evil, gains self-knowledge at the expense of his own happiness, a state symbolized by his former relationship with Phineas. A dominant theme in our literature, the death of innocence results from the growth of experience. From the time of breaking his leg on, Phineas's existence, both physically and symbolically, becomes a slow death; and as Gene progresses in self-knowledge, Phineas diminishes in force as individual while increasing as image and symbol. A central trait of Gene's makeup is revealed when he says:

I was used to finding something deadly in things that attracted me; there was always something deadly lurking in anything I wanted, anything I loved. And if it wasn't there, as for example with Phineas, then I put it there myself. (p. 92)

Contrast this outlook with that of Phineas, who, Gene observes, is "a poor deceiver, having had no practice," and in whom there "was no conflict except between athletes, something Greek-inspired and Olympian in which victory would go to whoever was the strongest in body and heart" (p. 144). In becoming a part of Phineas, though, Gene is made more aware of the difference between his own nature and Finny's, of the distinction between good and evil, of the contrast between illusion and reality.

Phineas, then, is the incarnation of the sporting hero before the fall, and in his world of the game there is no reminder of the real war going on in the outside world. When he is training Gene in his place for the '44 Olympics, Finny refutes Gene's observation that there will be no Olympics in 1944 with: "Leave your fantasy life out of this. We're grooming you for the Olympics, pal, in 1944." Phineas's flat denial of a schoolmaster's remark that "Games are all right in their place . . . but all exercise today is aimed of course at the approaching Waterloo" is not only indicative of his natural antipathy toward the authoritarian attitude of the academician, but also exemplifies his philosophy of a world without war or, in effect, a world of Edenic innocence. Perhaps the one activity in the novel that best illustrates Phineas's special genius for maintaining his sense of the way the world should be is his organization of a winter carnival, a kind of comic bacchanal performed in the dead of the New England winter. Because of it, Gene tells us that a "liberation" had been "torn from the gray encroachments of 1943, that an escape had been concocted, this afternoon of momentary, illusory, special and separate peace" (p.

128). In this womanless world of the Devon School for boys, Phineas's outlook asserts that the innocent state can be retained for as long as one can separate self from the man-made or obligatory realities that engulf it. However, Knowles implies that the seeds of discord are inherent in man, and we sense that it is only a matter of time before Finny's ideal world will be destroyed.

Paradoxically, it is Leper Lepellier's departure as "the Devon School's first recruit to World War II" that serves as the catalyst for Gene's encounter with self and prepares the way for the novel's denouement. Leper, viewed as an oddball by his classmates, is a romantic who finds personal identification with the simple realities of nature. Thus he is easily persuaded by a recruiting movie about the ski troops that at least one area of the war experience has its fine moments. However, Leper's sensitivity is undermined by his contact with the military, and after fleeing this alien existence for the security of his Vermont home, he sends for Gene, a friend he believes he can confide in. Now, though, with a more realistic perspective on life, Leper is moved to remind Gene of his evil act: " 'You always were a savage underneath. I always knew that only I never admitted it. . . . Like a savage underneath . . . like that time you knocked Finney out of the tree' " (p. 137). Leper, once an innocent himself, can now recognize evil for what it is, and Gene, although fearful of the truth, in yet another step toward self-awareness must return to Devon and Phineas to discover it for himself. Phineas, still holding onto his "separate peace," reveals to Gene an even more heightened contrast between illusion and reality. As Gene says:

> I found Finny beside the woods playing and fighting—the two were approximately the same thing to him—and I stood there wondering whether things weren't simpler and better at the northern terminus of these woods, a thousand

miles due north into the wilderness, somewhere deep into
the Arctic, where the peninsula of trees which began at
Devon would end at last in an untouched grove of pine,
austere and beautiful. (pp. 144-45)

Once again the sporting figure is identified with the
primal virtues of the wilderness, and standing on the
edge of Finny's snowball fight, Gene is hesitant as to
which side to join, his outlook reflecting his present state
of being—a Hegelian sense of self-alienation in which a
dialectical development controls the individual con-
sciousness and its progress from innocence to maturity.
Having become increasingly aware of two antithetical
ways of looking at experience, Gene, at this point, can
say of his own experience that he no longer needed a
"false identity; now I was acquiring, I felt, a sense of my
own real authority and worth, I had had many new experiences and I was growing up" (p. 148). Now, "growing up" demands the renunciation of the illusory world
of the child, and in terms of Gene's new experience,
Phineas and what he stands for must "die." During a
secret court in which Gene is placed on trial, the truth
of what actually happened in the tree is about to be revealed, but Finny, in one last effort to cling to the significance of his world, rushes from the room, falls down
a flight of stairs, and reinjures his leg. Complications set
in, and a few days later he is dead.

The death of Phineas is necessary to Gene's experience, because, even though Phineas had thought of
Gene as an "extension of himself," Gene's contact with
the real facts of existence compels a break with the way
of life Phineas represents. As Gene puts it concerning
Phineas's funeral: "I could not escape a feeling that this
was my own funeral, and you do not cry in that case" (p.
186). The death of innocence—the world of illusion and
Edenic reverie—has instilled in Gene a new way of "see-

ing." After one of his last talks with Phineas, Gene feels that he now has to "cope with something that might be called double vision," since the familiar objects of the campus have taken on a different appearance:

> I saw the gym in the glow of a couple of outside lights near it and I knew of course that it was the Devon gym which I entered every day. It was and it wasn't. There was something innately strange about it, as though there had always been an inner core to the gym which I had never perceived before, quite different from its generally accepted appearance. It seemed to alter moment by moment before my eyes, becoming for brief flashes a totally unknown building with a significance much deeper and far more real than any I had noticed before . . . and under the pale night glow the playing fields swept away from me in slight frosty undulations which bespoke meanings upon meanings, levels of reality I had never suspected before, a kind of thronging and epic grandeur which my superficial eyes and cluttered mind had been blind to before. (pp. 177-78)

Gene's new vision now focuses on complexities where there had formerly been a simple plain of existence equated with the innocent world of sporting endeavor. With the death of Phineas, then, Gene's essential encounter is complete, and at the end of the story he tells us:

> I was ready for the war, now that I no longer had any hatred to contribute to it. My fury was gone, I felt it gone, dried up at the source, withered and lifeless. Phineas had absorbed it and taken it with him, and I was rid of it forever. (p. 195)

Phineas, whose special attitude would have made him a casualty, escapes the disintegrating effect of war, whether it be between individuals or nations, escapes even the fact of losing his basic innocence and growing into a Christian Darling or a Rabbit Angstrom. The "separate peace" declared by Phineas is genuine, for as Gene observes in comparing Phineas with his other classmates:

> Only Phineas never was afraid, only Phineas never hated anyone. Other people experienced this fearful shock somewhere, this sighting of the enemy, and so began an obsessive labor of defense, began to parry the menace they saw facing them by developing a particular frame of mind. (p. 196)

In contrasting two complementary types of the sporting myth, *A Separate Peace* meaningfully dramatizes the dangers involved when the individual encounters this inner enemy, for it is a powerful and mysterious foe, one that demands a special kind of defense.

Like Phineas, Bruce Pearson of Mark Harris's *Bang the Drum Slowly* is an innocent type, but a Jack Keefe kind of innocent, who apparently commands little respect from his associates and who ironically knows that he is going to die. Unlike other sporting figures, Bruce has little status as a third-string catcher for the New York Mammoths (he is a big-league player however), while the story's narrator, Henry Wiggen, is a starting pitcher for the club. But we shall see that such a relationship is essential to the story's theme. Apparently feeling that Henry is the only person he can confide in, Bruce calls him during the off-season with the news that he is in a hospital in Rochester, Minnesota. Upon his arrival there, Henry discovers that Bruce is suffering from Hodgkin's disease and is given not too long to live, or, as Bruce puts it, "I am doomeded." Henry, who has never really been too friendly with Bruce before (he has strange habits like urinating in hotel washbowls and spitting tobacco juice out of the windows), feels compelled now to take Bruce under his wing. In order that Bruce not be dismissed from the club and may bow out gracefully,

Henry resolves not to tell anyone on the team of Bruce's condition during what may be his final season in baseball. It is this special knowledge of Bruce's tragic predicament that bring's about Henry's experience of encounter, for now he begins to observe things and events in a new light. Upon leaving Minnesota for Bruce's home in Georgia, Henry hears the station attendant who puts anti-freeze in their car remark that "This will last you a lifetime." Henry is moved to reflect on this statement:

> You would be surprised if you listen to the number of times a day people tell you something will last a lifetime, or tell you something killed them, or tell you they are dead. "I was simply dead," they say, "He killed me," "I am dying," which I never noticed before but now begun to notice more and more. I don't know if Bruce did. You never know what he notices nor what he sees, nor if he hears, nor what he thinks.[2]

As an innocent, Bruce is seemingly oblivious to the social significance of what goes on around him. His is an instinctive nature that finds itself most at home in familiar surroundings, and the closer they get to Bruce's home near Bainbridge, the more emotionally intense become his recollections of the playing fields of his youth. As Henry puts it, to Bruce "Georgia is a special place, different than all the others"—another reference to the great, good place that seems solidly imbedded in the subconscious of the sporting figure, a place where he "would of give most anything to settle down forever on . . . , never mind the fame and the glory, only give him time to live" (p. 27). Thus, during his stay at home, Bruce is moved to ask Henry a question that has perplexed the philosophers of all ages:

[2]Mark Harris, *Bang the Drum Slowly* (New York: Doubleday Anchor Books, 1962), p. 11.

"tell me why in hell I clumb to the top of the mill a million times and never fell down and killed myself, and why I never drowneded in the river, and why I never died in the war, and why I was never plastered by a truck but come clean through it all and now get this disease?" (p. 41)

It is a question, of course, that Henry cannot answer, but one that gives him an even more sensitive insight into Bruce's plight: "He stood a chance of living a long time yet, not too long but long enough, and I tried to keep him thinking of things yet ahead" (pp. 41-42). If, as usual, the theme of the dying athlete stresses the brevity of life, in this case it also lays emphasis on the unique worth and dignity of the individual. When Henry tells his wife, Holly, of Bruce's situation, he reveals that "she always liked him. She always said, 'Add up the number of things about him that you hate and despise, and what is left? Bruce is left' " (p. 14).

To Henry, the competitive nature of the game of baseball itself reflects the intrinsic worth of any human being, even when he exists as opponent: " 'The man you are facing is not a golf ball sitting there waiting for you to bash him. He is a human being, and he is thinking, trying to see through your system and trying to hide his own' " (p. 72). In answer to Bruce's admission that he has "never been smart," Henry praises those natural instincts of Bruce that distinguish him from other individuals:

"You been dumb on one count only. You left somebody tell you you were dumb. But you are not. You know which way the rivers run, which I myself do not know. . . .

"You know what is planted in the fields and you know the make of cows. Who in hell on this whole club knows one cow from the other? I could be stranded in the desert with 412 cows and die of thirst and hunger for all I know about a cow." (pp. 73-74)

Dutch Schnell, the manager of the Mammoths, is aware of something strange about the relationship between Henry and Bruce, and is fearful of what their actions might do to his team's pennant chances. A holdout at the beginning of the season, Henry, before signing, has a clause put into his contract insuring that he and Bruce "will stay with the club together, or else go together." Dutch is determined to get to the bottom of the matter, since he feels that his catching department is weak anyway. In fact, he hates putting Bruce in the lineup, because he always errs in receiving and giving signs. Consequently, Bruce is a kind of nonentity to Dutch, who never "spoke to him when he seen him around. But he carried him along. To him Bruce was a spare part rattling in the trunk that you hardly even remember is there between looks" (p. 78).

In this work, which owes so much to the Mark Twain-Ring Lardner vernacular tradition, Harris has used irony in such a controlled manner that he manages to avoid the pitfall of sentimentality. The drama of the story is heightened by the process of Bruce's slow death's being played out against the background of a championship pennant race, Henry's finest pitching record in several seasons, and Holly's giving birth to Henry's first child. The skillful interweaving of these events creates a poignant situation in which the significance of Bruce Pearson's role and identity is sharpened to its most meaningful extent. The meaning of life takes on more immediacy because of the fact of impending death. It should be noted also that Henry's position as a life insurance salesman during the off-season adds much to the basic framework of the story, where in the beginning he informs us that he has already sold Bruce a $50,000 policy, the kind Henry refers to as "North Pole coverage" because it "covers everything except sunstroke at the North Pole." It is the role of this insurance policy in *Bang the Drum Slowly* that affords us still another example of the strained relationship between sporting figure and woman.

Naïve, and lacking in self-awareness, Bruce has fallen in love with a prostitute named Katie, whom he wants to marry. Katie, who runs a lucrative business at her place, is not interested in marrying someone "dumb from the country," but she is interested in Bruce's insurance policy. Apparently aware of his dying condition, she urges him to change the beneficiary to her name and then she will marry him. Bruce presents her request to Henry a number of times, but Henry, wise to Katie's designs, always manages an excuse. He also successfully wards off Katie's temptations, one of which is a "golden lifetime pass" to her establishment. To Katie's observation that life is short, so "why not live it up a little?" Henry replies:

> "I do not know," I said, and that was true, for I did not. Do not ask me why you do not live it up all the time when dying is just around the corner, but you don't. You would think you would, but you don't. "I do not know why," I said. (p. 200)

Some of the other team members, who have always looked upon Bruce as a fall guy, begin to "rag" him concerning either his "pending" marriage with Katie or his unseemly relationship with Henry. Finally, in an attempt to curtail some of the jokes about Bruce, Henry tells Goose Williams about his condition. Goose is sworn to secrecy, but he tells his roommate, and after Bruce suffers an attack, Henry urges his teammates to let up on him. It is not long before the entire club learns of

Bruce's predicament. Their collective attitude at this point is akin to that of Henry's when he condemns his own selfish thoughts:

> When your roomie is libel to die any day on you you do not think about bonus clauses, and that is the truth whether anybody happens to think so or not. Your mind is on *now* if you know what I mean. You might tell yourself 100 times a day, "Everybody dies sooner or later," and that might be true, too, which in fact it is now that I wrote it, but when it is happening sooner instead of later you keep worrying about what you say *now*, and how you act *now*. There is no time to say, "Well, I been a heel all week but I will be better to him beginning Monday" because Monday might never come. (p. 139)

Now painfully aware of one individual's mortality and his role in life, the team begins to recognize Bruce's unique contribution to the success of their pennant drive. Although weak at detecting signs, Bruce is a dependable hitter, and Dutch feels compelled to put him in the lineup for this ability alone. The fact that Bruce is playing a position for which he is not suited (Henry attests to this fact throughout the novel) adds to his functional significance in the story. Furthermore, the juxtaposition of Bruce's plight with the devil-may-care attitude of his replacement, Piney Woods, lends emphasis to yet another irony of life—some individuals taunt the very image of death and still go on living. When he is not playing baseball, Piney gives Dutch gray hairs by driving motorcycles in such reckless fashion that one player remarks, "With all the ways of dying you would think a fellow would wait for them, not go out looking." But near the end of the season death comes looking for Bruce Pearson, and he finishes up on the bench as cadaverous in appearance as the image of the cowboy in

Piney's song, parts of which periodically appear in this section of the story:

> O bang the drum slowly and play the fife lowly,
> Play the dead march as they carry me on,
> Put bunches of roses all over my coffin,
> Roses to deaden the clods as they fall.

At the close of the novel, after Henry's having served as a "pallbear" at Bruce's funeral, his eulogy exists as a reminder that his encounter, or education in learning to respect the worth of the individual, is over:

> He was not a bad fellow, no worse than most and probably better than some, and not a bad ballplayer neither when they give him a chance, when they laid off him long enough. From here on in I rag nobody. (p. 224)

It is significant that both narrators of the novels examined in this section grow as individuals through their intimate relationship with the experience of the other, more tragic figures. *Bang the Drum Slowly* is infinitely more than a dirge or eulogy for a fallen sporting hero. It is a humanistic hymn that, in recognizing man's fallibility and mortality, also praises his identity in the common experience of all men.

The Agony of Rabbit Angstrom: The Search for a Secure Self

> To the athlete, every contest is a life and death struggle in the maintenance of the integrity of his own ego defenses.
> —Robert Boyle, *Sport–Mirror of American Life*

Both John Cheever and John Updike have turned out fictional works (Cheever a short story and Updike a novel) dealing with essentially the same problem that faces the latter-day version of the sporting hero. Cash Bentley of "O Youth and Beauty!" (1958) is a suburbanite husband with many worries, primarily financial. He has two children, lives in a "medium cost ranchhouse," and belongs to the country club, although he cannot afford it. While his is a marriage marked by dissension, Cash's biggest worry seems to stem from the growing realization that his hair is thinning and he is getting older. Although he still retains a slender figure and the "light and vigorous step that marked him as an athlete," Cash feels that the glory of his former identity as a track star is fading away. Unwilling to accept this fact, he attempts to recapture some measure of his past greatness by running hurdle races at parties and the country club. After plying himself with sufficient drink, Cash simply has chairs lined up as a hurdles course and proceeds to perform. "It was not exactly a race," writes Cheever, since Cash ran it alone, but it was extraordinary to see this man of forty surmount so many obstacles so gracefully."[3]

The irony of such a situation, as we shall also see in the case of Rabbit Angstrom, is that Cash, in his intense desire to preserve his ego, is seen to be much more competent as athlete than as responsible family man. Once again social demands deny expression to the narcissistic side of the sporting figure, and when Cash breaks a leg in one of his races, his crippled condition becomes symbolic of his distorted values as well as of his fear of loss of image. From this point on, symbols of disintegration and death abound:

He went into the kitchen late one night to make himself a sandwich, and when he opened the icebox door he noticed

[3]John Cheever, "O Youth and Beauty!" from *The Housebreaker of Shady Hill* (New York: Harper & Bros., 1958), p. 34.

a rank smell. He dumped the spoiled meat into the garbage, but the smell clung to his nostrils. (pp. 39-40)

Rummaging around in the attic for his old varsity sweater, Cash breaks "a spider web with his lips." In the city he spies an "old whore standing in a doorway [who] looked like a cartoon of Death." And later, at home, he notices that some faded roses from the garden have a "putrid, compelling smell." Then, in a lament closely akin to the tone of Updike's style in *Rabbit, Run,* Cash reflects on the meaning of his loss of image:

> He does not understand what separates him from these children next door. He has been a young man. He has been a hero. He has been adored and happy and full of animal spirits, and now he stands in a dark kitchen, deprived of his athletic prowess, his impetuousness, his good looks—of everything that means anything to him. He feels as if the figures in the next yard are the specters from some party in the past where all his tastes and desires lie, and from which he has been cruelly removed. . . . He is sick with longing. (p. 43)

Cash Bentley's peculiar kind of romantic longing is evidence of the neo-romantic state of mind that seeks to adjust reality to personal dreams. Symbolic of this quest is the close of the story, when Cash, apparently whole again, attempts another race. His wife holds the starter's pistol: "The pistol went off and Louise got him in midair. She shot him dead" (p. 46). The mobility of Cash Bentley has more meaning in terms of his romantic goal when his experience becomes immobile or "frozen," so to speak, for his quest to recapture the image of his former self is unattainable and doomed to failure. Symbolically, Cash's "pursuit" is arrested by death, the only real solution to his particular problem. Such a role of symbolic action plays an even more meaningful part in a novel like *Rabbit, Run* (1960).

The physical action of Rabbit Angstrom is integral to his story and pertinent to its purpose since his kind of mobility says more about his true nature than anything else in the novel. Thus, at the end—unable to choose between Janice, his alcoholic wife, or Ruth, the pickup whom he has got pregnant—Rabbit reacts in the only way he knows how: he runs. As expressed in another place:

> the choice of Rabbit's "running" as a central metaphor controlling the entire action of the novel is a masterly stroke. As an image stemming from Rabbit's athletic background, the act of running becomes ironically the mark of the passive man rather than that of the active individual. Thus, the act of running doubles as a comment on the one thing Rabbit knows he can do well in a world of uncertainty and as a comment on his failure to be a good husband. Moreover, it is a perfectly chosen metaphor because its implications apply so aptly to the modern condition at large and not just to Rabbit's predicament. By parallelling his hero's athletic past with his abortive present, Updike has enhanced as well as given purpose to the meaning of his writing. We discover that Rabbit as his high school team's star was not so much concerned with protecting his team's honor as he was his own.[4]

We are led to realize, then, that Rabbit's problem is deeper than his admission that "somewhere there was something better for him than listening to babies cry and cheating people in used-car lots.[5] Every action of his represents either an attempt to preserve his image from those threats that would imperil it or a desire to return to whatever can give him a sense of his former status and security. The irony of Rabbit's situation is furthered

---

[4]W. L. Umphlett, "Theme and Structure in John Updike's *Rabbit, Run*," *Laurel Review* 5 (Fall 1965): 36.

[5]John Updike, *Rabbit, Run* (New York: Crest Books, 1962), p. 225.

by the fact that no matter what action he takes to improve his lot, frustration and failure result.

Rabbit's fear of loss of image is brought out at the very beginning of the novel, when he engages in a pickup game of basketball with some grade school boys and thinks:

> You climb up through the little grades and then get to the top and everybody cheers; with sweat in your eyebrows you can't see very well and the noise swirls around you and lifts you up, and then you're out, not forgotten at first, just out, and it feels good and cool and free. You're out, and sort of melt, and keep lifting, until you become like to these kids just one more piece of sky of adults that hangs over them in town. . . . They've not forgotten him; worse, they never heard of him. (p. 9)

But this threat to his being is hardly passed when another presents itself, this one, the most formidable, in the person of his wife, whom he finds drunk at home and watching a Walt Disney show on television. The experience sickens him and provides the impetus for one of Rabbit's many "runs," this one a wild drive south which, in keeping with the sporting myth, is symbolic of his desire to escape complications and return to primitive simplicity:

> He wants to go south, down, down the map into orange groves and smoking rivers and barefoot women. It seems simple enough, drive all night through the dawn through the morning through the noon park on a beach take off your shoes and fall asleep by the Gulf of Mexico. Wake up with the stars above perfectly spaced in perfect health. (p. 25)

But urban imagery seems to dominate the unfolding highway, and the farther he drives the more perverted becomes the significance of the once-beckoning forest:

The land refuses to change. The more he drives the more
the region resembles the country around Mt. Judge. The
same scruff on the enbankments, the same weathered bill-
boards for the same insane products. At the upper edge of
his headlight beams the naked tree-twigs make the same
net. Indeed the net seems thicker now. (p. 32)

Rabbit's purposeful action is frustrated again, and on
the return home the athletic metaphor asserts itself
when Rabbit senses that now he

has broken through the barrier of fatigue and come into a
calm flat world where nothing matters much. The last
quarter of a basketball game used to carry him into this
world; you ran not as the crowd thought for the sake of the
score but for yourself, in a kind of idleness. (p. 35)

As in the game, Rabbit's life has evolved into a kind of
"last quarter," where the only thing that counts is running purely for the preservation of one's sense of ego.
Like Cash Bentley, Rabbit has developed a distorted
sense of values simply because life does not measure up
to the way he would like it to be. If a competitive game
can be thought of as a fantasy of life, then part of Rabbit Angstrom's personal tragedy is that he still lives in a
world where the issues of responsibility are determined
by the number of points he himself scores.

A similar situation is neatly dramatized in a short story
by Irwin Shaw called "Mixed Doubles," in which the
reasons for the marital difficulties of the story's two central figures are brought out in the playing of a tennis
match. As the match progresses, Jane Collins observes
that her husband, Stewart, her playing partner, has led a
life of form and gesture and that "his tennis was so
much like his life. Gifted, graceful, powerful, showy,
flawed, erratic."[6] At the close of the story, when Stewart

[6]Shaw, p. 235.

double faults, losing the match to their inferior opponents, and makes his final excuse, we realize that Stewart, like Rabbit, is also motivated to preserve ego status in spite of social priorities.

Rabbit's seeking out his old coach, the lecherous and dissipated Marty Tothero, for counsel is expressive of more than his desire to identify with a meaningful past; this perverse coach-player relationship is symbolic of Rabbit's failure to evaluate the significance of his actions. The advice Tothero offers Rabbit comes out in the form of coaching platitudes that emphasize the weaknesses of Rabbit's character and also illustrate the decline of authority in modern life. As a coach, Tothero says he has been concerned with developing the head, the body, and the heart. The head is for exercising the finer points of the game, while the body must be made hard through constant running. Players should "Run, run, run. Run every minute their feet are on the floor. You can't run enough." In respect to the heart, the good coach, says Tothero, should

> "Give the boys the will to achieve, I've always liked that better than the will to win, for there can be achievement even in defeat. Make them feel the . . . *sacredness* of achievement, in the form of giving our best. . . . A boy who has had his heart enlarged by an inspiring coach," he concludes, "can never become, in the deepest sense, a failure in the greater game of life."[7]

These cliché-ish comments from his old coach exist, then, as yet another side of the many-faceted athletic or game metaphor that controls, directs, and lends especial meaning to Rabbit's peculiar kind of abulia.

Paradoxically, sexual involvement to Rabbit represents both a threat to his image as well as a means of self-

[7]Updike, pp. 54-55.

definition. His relations with Janice apparently frustrated, he seeks a more vivid identity through his experiences with Ruth, whom he has met through Tothero. Updike records explicit sexual encounters between them, but Ruth, although a loser herself, is quick to perceive that her relationship with Rabbit outside of bed will lead to naught. To her he becomes nothing more than what he is—a self-oriented person who "just lived in his skin and didn't give a thought to the consequences of anything" (p. 125), which assessment turns out to be one of the more perceptive remarks of the novel. In reality, Rabbit's religious devotion to the act of sex is expressive of his own instinctive nature. Because every action of Rabbit's is instinctive (in keeping with his athletic nature and Updike's metaphorical intent), the intensity of sexual experience becomes equated with the once-intense physical action of the game. Even the sexual act, then, exists as a kind of "running" activity for Rabbit—an attempt to recapture that which was once so meaningful. Thus, as a victim of his own impulsive desires, Rabbit lives within the confines of a world wherein he is not only the star pointmaker, but the rulesmaker and final arbiter as well. His philosophy of life, if one may apply this designation to his attitude, appears to be based on the remark he makes to Ruth: "When I ran from Janice I made an interesting discovery . . . if you have the guts to be yourself . . . other people'll pay your price" (p. 125). Confined and restricted within the prison of his instinctive nature, then, Rabbit can never adjust his impulsive actions to the dictates of society. This conflict recurs throughout the novel, and, as one critic has pointed out, forms a basis for the novel's unity, which centers "around Rabbit's impulse for the natural and the consequences of the impulse."[8] The generic

[8]Gerry Brenner, "*Rabbit, Run:* John Updike's Criticism of the 'Return to Nature,' " *Twentieth Century Literature* 12 (April 1966): 3.

source for Rabbit's outlook is contained in a story Updike wrote in the 1950s called "Ace in the Hole," in which an ex-basketball player with domestic problems exists as a younger Rabbit. The same attitude persists in Updike's novel showing Rabbit approaching middle age, *Rabbit Redux* (1971).

Rabbit's dealings with Eccles, the minister who attempts to urge him back into a purposeful social pattern, show Rabbit as unable to comprehend what the institution of the church has to offer him and as therefore in the direct tradition of the sporting hero. Since "his feeling that there is an unseen world is instinctive,"[9] Christianity, even though it has been an integral part of his upbringing, is only something that one dresses up for on Sunday morning, as evidenced by his feelings the time he attends church after the first reconciliation with Janice:

> He hates all the people on the street in dirty everyday clothes, advertising their belief that the world arches over a pit, that death is final, that the wandering thread of his feelings leads nowhere. Correspondingly he loves the ones dressed for church. (p. 196)

Again the feeling is purely instinctive, something he recalls from boyhood. When Eccles reminds Rabbit that "You don't care about right or wrong; you worship nothing except your own worst instincts" (p. 112), he displays some lack of perceptiveness. For the truth of the matter is that for Rabbit, in following the lead of his instincts, *nothing* can be really bad, except, of course, that which would deny him existential fulfillment as, seemingly, his marriage does. In defense of his actions Rabbit is prompted to tell Eccles:

[9]Updike, p. 195.

I once played a game real well. I really did. And after you're first-rate at something, no matter what, it kind of takes the kick out of being second-rate. And that little thing Janice and I had going, boy, it was really second rate. (p. 90)

Christianity, then, is not a real experience for Rabbit, since it represents but another institutionalized force designed to curb his natural feelings. The ineffectuality of organized religion in regard to Rabbit's experience is dramatized in the clash of Eccles and Reverend Kruppenbach, whose conservative theological views contrast markedly with those of Eccles, tempered by the new psychology. But the viewpoint of either man of the church can offer no means of dealing with the basic nature of Rabbit, who, in his devotion to the religion of self,

has no taste for the dark, tangled, visceral aspect of Christianity, the *going through* quality of it, the passage *into* death and suffering that redeems and inverts these things, like an umbrella blowing inside out. He lacks the mindful will to walk the straight line of a paradox. (p. 147)

Like the seasons, Rabbit's pattern of behavior is cyclical, and we recognize his close feeling for nature when he obtains a job as a gardener, the point in the novel when he appears to feel most secure:

He loves folding the hoed ridge of crumbs of soil over the seeds. Sealed, they cease to be his. The simplicity. Getting rid of something by giving it. God himself folded into the tiny adamant structure . . . felt without words in the turn of the round hoe-handle in his palms. (p. 115)

Again the feeling is instinctive, and the primitive simplicity that is solace and consolation for the sporting hero becomes for Rabbit a temporary refuge from the entanglements of his life. As a recent study expresses it, "Rabbit still vaguely believes in the pastoral American Dream of eternal youth and transcendental harmony with nature."[10] But it is suggested throughout *Rabbit, Run* that modern society will not allow the individual a direct identification with nature. Updike skillfully manages this point through a meaningful blending of nature and urban imagery, the import of which implies that modern man's vision is blurred when he must distinguish real values in a natural environment. When Rabbit runs toward the forest after the burial of his baby daughter in the cemetery, his action seems symbolic of his desire to reassert his uncertain image after having been in the presence of death, the great antagonist of self. But the forest imagery is no longer equated with life and freedom of action. Instead, Rabbit's

> hands and face are scratched from plowing through the bushes and saplings that rim the woods. . . . The pine trees smother all other growth. Their brown needles muffle the rough earth with a slippery blanket; sunshine falls in narrow slots on this dead floor. It is dim but hot in here, like an attic; the unseen afternoon sun bakes the dark shingles of green above his head. Dead lower branches thrust at the level of his eyes. . . . As a kid he often went up through the woods. But maybe as a kid he walked under a magic protection that has now been lifted; he can't believe the woods were this dark then. They too have grown. Such an unnatural darkness, clogged with spider-fine twigs that linger his face incessantly, a darkness in defiance of the broad daylight whose sky leaps in jagged patches from treetop to treetop above him like a blue monkey.[11]

The lesson is plain. The demands of society are now of such consequence that they will never allow a return

[10]Larry E. Taylor, *Pastoral and Anti-Pastoral Patterns in John Updike's Fiction* (Carbondale: Southern Illinois University Press, 1971), p. 75.
[11]Updike, pp. 245-46.

to the primal innocence of a Natty Bumppo, oblivious to encroaching civilization. To pursue one's instinctive nature in order to project a secure image of self paradoxically results in death and disintegration. When Rabbit runs back to Ruth at the close of the novel, she calls him "Mr. Death," wandering around with "the kiss of death." Her ultimatum that he get out of her life enables him to see himself more clearly than he ever has before: "His hands and legs are suffused with a paralyzing sense of reality; his child is really dead, his day is really done, this woman is really sickened by him" (p. 251). Such awareness urges upon Rabbit the most basic of his athletic instincts: he runs, and the novel closes with another relevant use of the game metaphor as Rabbit reflects:

> Funny, how what makes you move is so simple and the field you must move in is so crowded he doesn't know, what to do, where to go, what will happen, the thought that he doesn't know seems to make him infinitely small and impossible to capture. Its smallness fills him like a great vastness. It's like when they heard you were great and put two men on you and no matter which way you turned you bumped into one of them and the only thing to do was pass. So you passed and the ball belonged to the others and your hands were empty and the men on you looked foolish because in effect there was nobody there. (p. 254)

In truth, Rabbit will never recapture his lost image; so he runs. It is this final "run" that thematically stands as the final judgment of his character and aesthetically brings the novel full circle.

Roy Hobbs and the Quest for the American Dream

> baseball is not only part of the American mythology but . . . sports are themselves mythological or pseudo-religious in their appeal and their importance.
>   —Otto Friedrich, *Ring Lardner*

If by the term *natural* we wish to imply that which is derived from or defined by nature, it is fitting that I close the neo-romantic section of the sporting myth's function in American literature by examining a work that draws on the resources of traditional myth not only to enhance the meaning of the sporting hero's role but also to pull together in one work the various themes apparent in modern fiction. In *The Natural* (1952), Bernard Malamud has created a hero whose experience, even though it parallels that of various heroes of traditional myth, represents a composite of the sporting hero's distinguishing characteristics. Like the representative hero of the sporting myth, Roy Hobbs

is impelled by dreams of a noble future, of love and children, of the pastoral idyls of his childhood, and, at the same time, haunted by the nightmare awareness of their impossibility, of their irrevocable loss.[12]

But it is the instincts of the sporting hero that force Roy's essential encounter and help express awareness of the great distance between dream and reality in American experience. In fact, the novel is structured so that Roy's experience is illustrative of the story's major theme: if one is to pursue a dream, he must pay the price for its pursuit.

In a psychological sense the game of baseball is a characteristically significant sport for a writer to use in conveying action symbolic of American experience because in this game so much is dependent on individual effort within a team situation. In fact, the game's "essentially democratic nature," with its "record of day-by-day failure or accomplishment,"[13] reflects the nature of

---

[12]Jonathan Baumbach, *The Landscape of Nightmare: Studies in the Contemporary American Novel* (New York: New York University Press, 1965), p. 110.

[13]Cozens and Stumpf, p. 51.

American life itself, a situation that Robert Coover uses to great advantage in his *The Universal Baseball Association, Inc.* (1968). One of Roy's teammates puts it aptly: "Anything can happen to you in this game. Today you are on top and tomorrow you will be on your way out to Dubuque." Roy Hobbs himself can verify the truth of this observation, since he spends fifteen years in the bush leagues before making the big time, and even when he does, he discovers that his position is never secure. However, Roy's years as a minor leaguer are integral to interpreting and understanding the meaning and interrelationship of the two major divisions of the story.

When we first meet Roy, he is a young ballplayer, a naïf obsessed by the dream of success, on his way to his first major-league assignment, and, as he expresses it, with "my whole life ahead of me." At the very beginning, too, the nature of Roy's preoccupation is introduced when we are told of a

> dream he could never shake off . . . of him standing at night in a strange field with a golden baseball in his palm that all the time grew heavier as he sweated to settle whether to hold on or fling it away.[14]

As a sporting hero of contemporary times, Roy pursues a dream that has engendered within his own mind an irreconcilable conflict between his essential innocence, as suggested by the novel's recurring references to the forest and his lost boyhood, and the confrontation of experience that the challenge of his goal demands. His feelings are appropriately expressed when he looks out of the train window and reflects:

> Gosh, the size of the forest. He thought they had left it for

[14]Bernard Malamud, *The Natural* (New York: Dell Books, 1965), p. 8.

good yesterday and here it still was. As he watched, the trees flowed together and so did the hills and clouds. He felt a kind of sadness, because he had lost the feeling of a particular place. Yesterday he had come from somewhere, a place he knew was there, but today it had thinned away in space . . . and he felt he would never see it again.

The forest stayed with them, climbing hills like an army, shooting down like waterfalls. As the train skirted close in, the trees leveled out and he could see within the woodland the only place he had been truly intimate with in his wanderings, a green world shot through with weird light and strange bird cries, muffled in silence that made the privacy so complete his inmost self had no shame of anything he thought there, and it eased the body-shaking beat of his ambitions. (p. 18)

During a layover on the trip Roy passes his first test of experience by striking out "Whammer" Wambold, the leading hitter in the American League, who has been taunting Roy because of his rookie outlook. With this feat he wins over Harriet Bird, the beautiful "enchantress" he has met on the trip, but Roy is still too naïve to discern the spell she has cast over him, and with her entering his life the trees of the forest become "tormented . . . fronting the snaky lake they were passing, trees bent and clawing, plucked white by icy blasts from the black water, their bony branches twisting in many a broken direction" (p. 26). Harriet, in fact, refers to herself as a "twisted tree," and when they arrive in Chicago, where Roy is to join his team, her feminine role of denying Roy a chance to achieve his goal represents the harsh realities of life with which innocence is ill-equipped to cope. In the surrealistic scene in the hotel room, Roy, who thinks he has come for a romantic assignation with Harriet, is instead shot by her with a silver bullet:

He sought with his bare hands to catch it, but it eluded him and, to his horror, bounced into his gut. A twisted dagger of smoke drifted up from the gun barrel. Fallen on one knee he groped for the bullet, sickened as he moved, and fell over as the *forest* flew upward, and she, making muted noises of triumph and despair, danced on her toes around the stricken hero. (p. 33) (Italics mine)

The action is purely symbolic, and with Harriet's gesture and Roy's accompanying loss of innocence, this section of the novel comes to a close. Roy is condemned to spend the next fifteen years of his life wandering from one bush-league team to another, searching out a meaning for his quest.

Critical reception of *The Natural* has been mixed, ranging from Ihab Hassan's accusation that the story "fails ultimately to make itself comprehensible"[15] to another critic's belief that the work is "an accomplished literary performance."[16] Marcus Klein sees *The Natural* as a "deliberate and an artful novel. Roy, the would-be king of the diamond, is more than he is. He is also Achilles before Troy, and he is the Grail Knight at the Castle, and for a moment at the beginning he is young David and also the son who must replace the father."[17] The mythical parallels are obvious in many places,[18] and while they help inform meaning within the novel itself, the various references to classical lore can confuse and distort the overall meaning of the story. On the other hand, if we consider Roy Hobbs as another hero in the tradition of the sporting myth, we are in an advantageous position to arrive at a clearer reading of the novel's basic intent. It is simple enough to parallel Pop Fisher, the disen-

[15]Hassan, p. 162.

[16]Helen Weinberg, *The New Novel in America: the Kafkan Mode in Contemporary Fiction* (Ithaca: Cornell University Press, 1970), p. 170.

[17]Marcus Klein, *After Alienation: American Novels in Mid-Century* (Cleveland: World Publishing Co., 1962), p. 256.

[18]For an interesting discussion of the Homeric parallels, see Norman Podhoretz, "Achilles in Left Field," *Commentary* 15 (March 1953): 321-26.

chanted manager of the New York Knights, with the Fisher King of fertility ritual, for as Pop remarks before the arrival of Roy: "It's been a blasted dry season. No rains at all. The grass is worn scabby in the outfield and the infield is cracking. My heart feels as dry as dirt for the little I have to show for all my years in the game."[19] But in accordance with the sporting myth, Pop Fisher exists as another authority figure whose main function has been to impose artificiality and sterility on the natural. On the surface his intentions appear good: to make the Knights into world champions. Underneath, he wants to compensate for the time, years before in the World Series, when he had fallen down rounding third with the winning run. But not until Roy arrives, proclaiming through his remarkable ability a return to the natural, do the Knights become pennant contenders. Even so, Roy must overcome the blind authoritarianism of his manager as well as the protestations of the league's leading hitter before he can prove himself as a player and restore order to a team that holds "the record of the most consecutive games lost in the whole league history, the most strikeouts, the most errors" (p. 43).

Roy's relationship to the game of baseball parallels that of his past relationship with nature, reminiscent of a time when he could feel a surer sense of identity. Because of Roy's inner conflict between a return to primal unity and the pursuit of a dream, he is presented, in the manner of the traditional sporting hero, as a man in motion. When he first reports to Pop Fisher in the Knights' dugout, we are told that

> although he was sitting here on this step he was still in motion. He was traveling (on the train that never stopped). His self, his mind, raced on and he felt he hadn't stopped

[19]Malamud, pp. 34-35.

going wherever he was going because he hadn't arrived. (p. 36)

In this story the image of the train is used in much the same manner as it is in Thomas Wolfe's writings, as a symbol of wandering and unfulfilled promise. So when Roy finally hits the majors at the age of thirty-four, when most baseball careers are either over or waning, he can reflect:

> It was different than he had thought it would be. So different he almost felt like walking out, jumping back on a train, and going wherever people went when they were running out on something. Maybe for a long rest in one of those towns he had lived in as a kid. Like the place where he had that shaggy mutt that used to scamper through the woods, drawing him after it to the deepest, stillest part, till the silence was so pure you could crack it if you threw a rock. (p. 40)

Roy still carries a symbol of his affinity with nature, his bat Wonderboy, capable of wondrous feats and carved out of a tree where he had lived. As a symbol of original innocence the bat is white, which Roy refers to as its "true color." Later, when he undergoes a severe slump after breaking many records, Roy is advised to change bats; but significantly he says the problem is in himself and not in the bat. It is a feeling that will precipitate Roy's experience of encounter, and even though he has set many new records, "he felt he had nothing of value yet to show for what he was accomplishing, and in his dreams he still sped over endless miles of monotonous rail toward something he desperately wanted" (p. 72). In *You Can't Go Home Again* (1940), Thomas Wolfe, fascinated by the mobility of the train, remarks that to the American it seems that experience becomes fixed only when he is in motion. Despite his sense of frustration, the meaning of motion or mobility is important to Roy's experience, as it is to all heroes of the sporting myth:

> He felt contentment in moving. It rested him by cutting down the inside motion—that which got him nowhere, which was where he was . . . , or where his ambitions were and he was chasing after. Sometimes he wished he had no ambitions—often wondered where they had come from in his life, because he remembered how satisfied he had been as a youngster, and that with the little he had had—a dog, a stick, an aloneness he loved (which did not bleed him like his later loneliness), and he wished he could have lived longer in his boyhood. This was an old thought with him. (p. 93)

The sense of aloneness that was a unique part of his lost boyhood is an essential part of the real quest of Roy Hobbs. His legacy is a natural sense of integrity, as illustrated by his refusal to be hypnotized along with his other teammates so as to improve their playing. But Roy's immediate problem is the same as that of other sporting heroes who find themselves divorced from their natural environment. He can no longer perceive true values. His predicament is clearly defined through his relationship with the women in his life, Memo Paris and Iris Lemon.

Memo is the Harriet Bird or sorceress of the second part of the novel. In love with Bump Baily, the league's leading hitter and Roy's antagonist, she is symbolic of those distorted values that Roy allows to undermine his quest. In fact, Pop, her uncle, tells Roy that "there is some kind of whammy in her that carries her luck to other people. That's why I would like you to watch out and not get too tied up with her" (p. 72). But after Bump's death and Roy's replacing him, he becomes very much involved with Memo despite his feeling that she is "too complicated." Her hold over him is such that she

becomes a symbol of the death of his inherently innocent nature. Out on a date with her, Roy allows her to
drive his car, and he begins to reflect:

> The white moonlight shot through a stretch of woods
> ahead. He found himself wishing he could go back some-
> where, go home, wherever that was. As he was thinking
> this, he looked up and saw in the moonlight a boy coming
> out of the woods, followed by his dog. Squinting through
> the windshield, he was unable to tell if the kid was an illu-
> sion thrown forth by the trees or someone really alive. . . .
> Roy yelled to Memo to slow down in case he wanted to
> cross the road. Instead, the car shot forward so fast the
> woods blurred, the trees racing along like shadows in weak
> light, then skipping into black and white, finally all black
> and the moon was gone. (pp. 97-98)

Roy is sure that Memo has run over the boy, but he can
find no trace of the body. Even so, Roy imagines from
this point on that a black car is pursuing him, and the
meaning of the imagery is obvious. Expulsion from
Edenic innocence is death, and like Harriet Bird, who
had cut Roy down "in the very flower of his youth,"
Memo Paris is really another reminder of his lost innocence. Thus we sense that the boy in Roy's imagination,
who "lay broken-boned and bleeding in a puddle of
light, with no one to care for him or whisper a benedic-
tion upon his lost youth" (p. 102), is really Roy Hobbs
himself.

After his night with Memo, Roy appears to be under
another spell, for despite his batting records he enters a
terrible slump. It is not until Iris Lemon comes into his
life with her enduring faith in his ability that he returns
to his former self. On first meeting Iris, Roy feels that
"in her wide eyes he saw something which caused him to
believe she knew what life was like," in contrast to
Memo, who is now "remote, even unreal" (pp. 120-21).

Iris, unlike the standard woman-type of the sporting myth, has learned the meaning of endurance and suffering through her own experience, and thereby possesses the power to diagnose Roy's problem. She tells him why she stood up for him when he suffered his slump: "I felt that if you knew people believed in you, you'd regain your power." She also reminds Roy that he has a special identity as a hero: "Without heroes we're all plain people and don't know how far we can go." Their function, she continues, is "to be the best and for the rest of us to understand what they represent and guide ourselves accordingly" (p. 123). Roy begins to realize his sporting-hero status, but he still feels that he has not gotten out of baseball and life what he has put into them. Iris still has advice for him when he indulges in self-pity:

> "why did it always have to happen to me? What did I do to deserve it?"
> "Being stopped before you started?"
> He nodded.
> "Perhaps it was because you were a good person?"
> "How's that?"
> "Experience makes good people better."
> She was staring at the lake.
> "How does it do that?"
> "Through their suffering."
> "I had enough of that," he said in disgust.
> "We have two lives, Roy, the life we learn with and the life we live with after that. Suffering is what brings us toward happiness." (pp. 125-26)

It is Roy's tragic mistake that he believes realization of the Dream itself brings "happiness" and not what one undergoes in search of it. Hence his weakness for confusing true values, as illustrated by his forsaking Iris and returning to Memo. In reality, Iris is too domesticated for the sporting experience, even though Roy's continued

relationship with Memo brings him into deeper involvement with an alien background, a predicament that
eventually brings about his tragic downfall.

As an authority figure and natural antagonist of Roy
Hobbs, Judge Goodwill Banner is supremely symbolic of
the duplicity of institutions in the sporting myth. Not
only is he the owner of the New York Knights, with the
final word as to player trades and salaries, but he lives
permanently detached in a dark tower high above
Knights Field. When Roy first approaches the Judge
about a raise in salary, he is quick to note characteristics
that emphasize the inherent duplicity of the Knights'
owner. Living in a darkened office whose floor is
slanted, he is given to quoting pious platitudes, which he
offers as remedy for any problem. To Roy's request for
an increase in salary to which he is certainly entitled, the
Judge tells him that the love of money is the root of all
evil. He elaborates further on this bit of homiletic wis-
dom by informing Roy that wealth-seeking can pervert
one's values. The irony of Judge Banner's reminding
Roy to shun material gain is that it underscores the fact
of the breakdown of value in the world of authority. For
the Judge, as a symbol of this world, is used in the same
manner as all authority figures who appear in literature
of the sporting myth—to emphasize the sporting hero's
state of alienation when confronted by the demands of
authoritarianism. Thus Roy's request for recognition for
his contribution to the Knights' success goes unheeded,
and he is compelled to leave the Judge's presence with
the admonition to "resist all evil" ringing in his ears. But
still chasing a dream and thinking of his and Memo's future, Roy accepts the Judge's bribe offer to throw the
game that will decide the league championship. Judge
Banner, who, of course, is not so much interested in
winning the championship as he is in making a great

deal of money out of the situation, exists by a deceptive and perverted code of values that warps and undermines Roy's outlook. Because Roy cannot cope with what the Judge stands for, he sells out.

Another factor affecting Roy's loss of integrity is that he has not learned the meaning of suffering that one must endure in the pursuit of a dream, those values derived from the lesson learned by Ike McCaslin or Santiago, for example. Thus he can turn his back on Iris, who has learned self-knowledge through suffering, and pursue Memo, who admits that she is "afraid to be poor," and that she must have everything that goes with material success. Gus Sands, the bookie and rival for Memo's hand, is a lesser Judge Banner ("He belonged in the dark with the Judge") who first suggests a bribe to Roy: "Say the word, slugger, and you can make yourself a nice pile of dough quick." The idea is repulsive to Roy at first, but fearful that his dream with Memo will be destroyed, he comes to an agreement with the Judge, who, along with Memo, is aware of Roy's feeling of insecurity and takes advantage of it.

True to the sporting myth, the symbolic scene in which Roy seeks sexual consummation with Memo results in his immolation and ensuing loss of strength. It is the cue for Iris's return, and his discovery that she is pregnant by him renews his love for her, but it is too late to redeem his personal honor even though he now sees the error of his ways. Batting in the championship game, he breaks Wonderboy, eventually strikes out, and loses the game. But having taken an important step in self-knowledge, Roy now has a clearer picture of himself in relationship to his dream. He buries Wonderboy, with the hope that "it would take root and become a tree," and takes out his vengeance on Gus and the Judge. No longer is he enchanted by Memo, who, like Harriet, attempts to shoot him, but is foiled. Stripped of his records and much of his self-esteem, Roy Hobbs now goes forth with a sense of humility and a self-awareness he has never had before. As he himself puts it: ". . . I never did learn anything out of my past life, now I have to suffer again" (p. 190).

The experience of Roy Hobbs informs us that there is actually no such thing as the realization of a dream; there can only be the satisfaction of working toward it in the manner of the sporting hero whose experience is involved in nature. In further paradox we discover through Roy's experience that the penalty for lack of self-knowledge is suffering; yet, through suffering, the individual comes to a fuller understanding of self. *The Natural*, because of its complex interweaving of the major themes of American experience, stands as one of the most intricate and complete expressions of the sporting myth in American literature.

Epilogue: Some Recent Trends and Variations

Literary heroes dramatize the moral texture of a country. Creations of the imagination, they embody the unspoken ideals, the undesired terrors, the dream life and the existence of their readers. Heroes represent a people, and by discovering the meaning of their character, by returning to the roots of their behavior, we discern the moral figure in the tapestry of a nation.

—Theodore L. Gross, *The Heroic Ideal in American Literature*

Even though the Frontier dwelt on in classic American literature is no more, the concept of the wilderness and its challenges still haunts us as a people. For this reason the role of the sporting hero in our future literature will continue to express itself as it has in the past—through our sense of mobility as it is focused through the encounter experience. Because we are living in an age that increasingly stresses leisure as value, our present sense of mobility is being modified as well as tested. We know that leisure can confine instead of free unless it is utilized to expand human capabilities, and paradoxically, as more leisure time becomes available, the so-called "sporting" individual seems to retreat into the role of spectator rather than be a participant. It may be that there are literary techniques to be developed and lessons to be learned from such a function, for the twentieth-century American who identifies with sport, even as active participant, is really a spectator of himself. In this section we shall examine evidence of this trend.

In fiction of recent years, especially since 1965, innovative experimentation with the concept of the sporting hero has led us down various avenues of expression and comment about the modern world. Problems once reserved for or expressed through the experience of other literary types now take on form and substance through a writer's unique handling of the American sporting experience to make either a direct or oblique statement about contemporary life. For example, in the most recent versions of the encounter with society, it is interesting to observe the emergence of the basketball player as a hero-type reflecting the writer's vision of societal problems.

One important reason for this development is that basketball has surpassed boxing as a more significant sport offering the participant a way out of the ghetto or system. Because it can be played in a relatively small area and requires very little equipment, basketball is *the* ghetto sport and the most urbanized of our team sports. With the influx of black people to our major cities since the war years, the pickup game of the city streets and schoolyards has generated enough talented players that today the college and professional games appear to be dominated by the black man. As a sport, too, the game of basketball, with its opportunity for loose, lyrical play seems a fitting vehicle of expression for the black man and his natural flair for showmanship as well as his sense of action as recurrent rhythm. In a more general sense, basketball has appeal to the writer because as an indigenous American game it epitomizes something of the American sense of mobility, with its emphasis on continuous attack, even on defense, and the challenge of almost constant man-to-man confrontation.

In Jay Neugeboren's *Big Man* (1966), the symbolic characteristics of the game are used to dramatize the social encounter of a black basketball player who has been mixed up with the college fix scandals of the early 1950s. Both as a black man in American society and also as a type of the sporting hero, Mack Davis exists as a literary character whose function is both ironic and symbolic. As a result his role is fraught with implications of the sporting myth.

Because of his involvement in the fixes of five years previous, Mack, at least on the surface, appears to have lost the aura of innocence that identifies the usual sporting hero. Yet his perceptive girlfriend, Willa, recognizes the immature streak in his personal makeup and keeps referring to him as a "big baby." Like Iris Lemon of *The Natural*, Willa has learned a great deal about life through suffering, and her tomboyish airs (she even plays as a regular on Mack's amateur team) as well as her constructive criticism of Mack's personal life show her as contributing to his growth toward self-awareness. At one point she tells him: "When you gonna stop waiting for somebody to come give you something and go out and do something yourself."[1] In such a remark Willa has hit on Mack's basic problem, for actually he is a fallen innocent who has lost his way and cannot act in a societal sense.

The only way that Mack can identify with the innocent times before the fall is through playing his schoolyard

[1] Jay Neugeboren, *Big Man* (Boston: Houghton, Mifflin Co., 1966), p. 206.

pick-up games. Throughout the novel the city schoolyard is pictured as Mack's great, good place, affording him the only experience in which he can become "real loose." Mack's feeling about it is that, no matter how big you make it—in high school, college, or the pro's—"it never compares with being king of your own school yard" (pp. 58-59). Having been exploited by the system of college sports and the gambling scandals, Mack Davis finds himself on a blacklist that has entrapped him somewhere between the idyllic world of the schoolyard and his dream of realizing himself as a successful professional player. Ben Rosen, the sports writer who feels that Mack has been victimized and starts a newspaper campaign to clear his name, tells him that his situation is similar to that of the Jew: "No place to go. You are able, qualified, free of sin—but the league has put the mark of Cain on you" (p. 99). Consequently, Mack keeps drifting back to the schoolyard and its close-knit hierarchy of hero worship. At least he has a certain amount of status here, that sense of achievement any sporting hero finds difficult to be without. Rosen himself recognizes the significance of the schoolyard when he remarks to Mack:

> "Every basketball player, be he the world's best or the world's worst, lives for his schoolyard. It's where he grows, where he lives out his youth, where he finds his glory. Maybe not for you as much as for my generation. For us it was an Eden!" (p. 83)

The penalty for Mack's inability to relate to society is suspended mobility—the "disease" familiar to most heroes of urban background. His attempt to relate is brought out rather dramatically toward the end of the novel when he turns down offers to become a fixer himself. In fact, he is ready to play ball with Rosen in order to get himself reinstated in the professional ranks, but the grounds for a case fall through, and the system wins out again. There is no place for Mack to go except back to the schoolyard, and the novel ends with Mack and his younger brother getting into another pick-up game: "We back in the big-time. Nobody gonna beat me and Ronnie. We gonna take on all comers" (p. 213). True to his understanding of the sporting code, Mack Davis can derive some sense of integrity in playing "the game" as he knows it should be played through his schoolyard experience.

In another recent novel we observe a basketball player performing as he thinks he should but for a different purpose. In the 1971 edition of *Drive, He Said,* Jeremy Larner draws a surrealistic picture of the basketball player as dropout, from not only society but the game itself, in order to criticize a warped, materialistic culture that has apparently lost sight of meaningful values. Hector Bloom, like Roy Hobbs of *The Natural,* has a somewhat mythical background and significance, for he is described as a "half-hick, half-Jew, lefthanded neurotic basketball player from the green hills of California."[2] Having come East on an athletic scholarship, Hector finds himself a pawn of the system, and his dream of true glory is shattered as he searches for meaning and identity in a world gone mad over materialistic standards. Hector, retaining his essential innocence, holds to the code of the sporting hero by attempting to thwart the edicts of the Establishment through practicing a personal code of conduct, which reinforces the novel's basic theme: the impossibility and absurdity of experiencing true identity or individuality in the modern world.

In Larner's world, dream and actuality merge, and at times it becomes difficult to distinguish between the two,

[2]Jeremy Larner, *Drive, He Said* (New York: Bantam Books, 1971), p. 21.

this situation lending to the meaning of the writer's technique in this work—the purposeful distortion of reality to project an attitude toward life. If reality is absurd, Larner seems to suggest, then fantasy may be closer to true experience. With the world on the brink of a catastrophic war at the novel's beginning, we are informed that Hector is suffering from a basic fear of the sporting hero: "The thought of death and obliteration had utterly unstrung young Hector Bloom. He had taken himself into a dream from which he couldn't wake, a dream of obligation and striving" (p. 2). Hector "dreams" he is an All-America basketball star playing before a national television audience, but the impending war and the authoritarian stance of his cliché-spouting coach keep intruding on his quest for meaningful identity, and when the game is over we learn that "This game was not a dream, it was [Hector's] life" (p. 8). By extension, life itself, according to Larner's vision, is like a nightmarish game in which the performance of the individual becomes a horrendous ordeal in which his identity and sense of integrity are subject to a variety of systematic onslaughts.

Put on the defensive, Hector establishes a sporting attitude and life-style that are symbolic of his desire to maintain his sense of personal being in the face of forces that would apparently destroy it. All his actions are anti-establishment and therefore in the finest tradition of the sporting hero. He does not even live with the other scholarship athletes. Instead, he lives in a caretaker's room beneath the college gymnasium with his friend Gabriel Reuben, self-styled revolutionary. Gabriel's underground role and the fact that he holds a work scholarship stoking the gym's furnace lend him a kind of demonic significance in the novel. Actually, Gabriel sees in Hector's response to the world an active symbol of his own intent to overthrow the System. During practice sessions Hector plays alone, much to the chagrin of his "Fighting Coach," and as a result he is "the only player in Coach Bullion's career who remained absolutely unaffected by his coaching" (p. 103). As an advocate of the "loose lost Negro" style of play as opposed to the Coach's "white-boss" style, Hector plays for himself to assert self. He breaks a social taboo by dating a professor's wife. He hobnobs with pot-smoking radicals who believe "you've got to make it your own way, like Hector Bloom plays ball!" (p. 27). Even Hector's classroom experiences place him in a unique category, as revealed through his disagreements with his self-assured humanities professor. At a wild party he debates with a munitions magnate about the meaning of life in America, their dialogue emphasizing the wide gulf between dream and fact in modern life. At the same party, though, Olive, the professor's wife with whom he has been having an affair, rebuffs him: "Get away from me, you huge boy, you naïf!" Olive, of course, is the symbol of the sophisticated and Establishment-oriented life alien to the sporting hero, and even though Hector thinks himself in love with her, she naturally disowns him in the end.

Hector Bloom is really Melville's Bartleby in the guise of an athlete, and at one point, when Coach Bullion is exhorting his players to work hard, Hector echoes the classic remark of Bartleby by telling the Coach, "I prefer not to" (p. 105). Whether or not to play in the Big Game is the question that Hector discovers he must reply to and that provides the focus for his essential encounter. At first he runs, but his sojourn in the alien city can provide no answer:

Most of the faces were subway faces, grey and set in bitterness. Among cars in the streets, the children played savagely, with bottle caps and rubber balls and chalk and tin cans. They were desperately alive yet, but in automatic distrust they turned from Hector's advances. (p. 117)

So Hector plays in the Big Game, but plays it his own disinterested way, if only to "lose" while winning and thereby retain some sense of individuality. The irony of Hector Bloom's quest is similar to that of Prewitt's in *From Here to Eternity.* In the attempt to maintain personal integrity within a system that measures success by what individual performance contributes to the whole, true identity is sacrificed and oftentimes lost.

Despite its decline in popularity as a participant sport, boxing still remains an effective mode through which a writer can describe or criticize societal problems or entrapment within a system. An excellent example of this tradition is Leonard Gardner's *Fat City* (1969), a novel in which second-rate fighters are used to portray a third-rate way of life in urbanized society. In fact, the very title itself identifies the city as enemy, a reality brought out right from the beginning of the book when we are introduced to Billy Tully's bleak background:

> From his window he looked out on the stunted skyline of Stockton—a city of eighty thousand surrounded by the sloughs, rivers and fertile fields of the San Joaquin River delta—a view of business buildings, church spires, chimneys, water towers, gas tanks and the low roofs of residences rising among leafless trees between absolutely flat streets. Along the sidewalk under his window, men passed between bars and liquor stores, cafés, secondhand stores and walk-up hotels.[3]

Throughout the novel, imagery of the city is juxtaposed against nature imagery—in fact, dominates it as if to

[3]Leonard Gardner, *Fat City* (New York: Dell Books, 1972), p. 7.

symbolize the subjection of the story's characters to the impersonal system within which they find themselves.

Billy Tully, drifter, is an ex-fighter fearful of growing old, who likes to think he still has a chance for a comeback. He spars with a young hopeful named Ernie Munger, whose promising talent he praises as an extension of himself "in order to go on believing in his body." Ernie Munger, as a younger Tully and a sporting hero, feels that he has "joined the company of men" when he becomes a member of a stable of second-rate club fighters. Living at home, Ernie endures a life remindful of that of Hemingway's Krebs, the kind of life that denies him mobility and freedom of identity. But even his training program, designed to make him a better fighter, symbolizes the dominance of the societal over the natural:

> Zipped up in his leather jacket, each fist squeezing a small rubber ball, he ran along the dirt road past burst mattresses, water heaters, fenders, sodden cartons, worn-out tires and rusty cans strewn down the steep bank. At the shore rocked bottles and driftwood, blackened tules, papers and occasionally a reeking belly-up fish. Gulls turned in the gray sky and stood on piles across the channel. . . . As larks rose with flashes of yellow from the dead weeds and wild grass, sailed ahead, landed, sang their six tremulous notes, hushed and flew up once more, he came unflaggingly on, feeling he would never tire. (p. 30)

Waste products of the "fat city" pervade the natural environment at every turn, but the biggest waste of all, this novel seems to suggest, is the human potential.

Unable to express and realize his own potential in such a background, Ernie meets a girl with whom his relationship is at first purely sexual but whom he eventually marries—out of no more reason than the feeling of "obligations." He has not been married long, though, before the special attitude of the sporting hero toward woman begins to haunt him:

> It was not comprehension that he wanted, only her aware-ness that he was not like anyone she had known before. But it was as if what distinguished him was what she did not perceive. At times as he lay in bed listening to her breath-ing, a fear came over him that after marriage death was the next major event. (p. 94)

Married and working as a gas station attendant, Ernie can now cling only to his dream of being a great fighter as a way out—the dream of Billy Tully.

Tully, in the meantime, has been working as a fruit picker and field hand to obtain money to live on. This kind of work represents his only contact with nature, but the relationship is unnatural because of the back-breaking labor involved and the inevitable contacts with co-workers who are derelicts, products of the city and perversions of humanity. A central symbol of the novel and one that meaningfully points out the disparity be-tween the natural and the distorted is the action taken by the city to cut the trees down that shade the park area where the winos hang out. Their retreat gone, now their behavior is open for the world to see.

Tully, separated from his wife but still searching for some kind of meaningful existence, is haunted by her because she reminds him of his days of glory as a fighter. In desperation he takes up with a woman he meets in a bar. She, of course, represents entrapment to him, even after the sexual act:

> He lay quietly, oppressed by a sense of dwindling life, of his youth dwindling away as he rested beside a woman he should never have known, here so far off the course he knew should have been his that he wondered with panic if it had been lost forever. (p. 112)

In a quest for rebirth, Tully attempts a comeback in the ring, but the relationship with his woman brings upon him an acute state of bodily awareness and "an agony of confinement. He was balked. His life seemed near its end. In four days he would be thirty" (p. 119). When he leaves the woman, he wins a fight, and with the self-confidence and brimming optimism of a reborn sporting hero, he assesses himself: "He felt whole, self-sufficient, felt his life had at last opened up and that now nothing stood between him and the future's infinite possibilities" (p. 157).

But Tully gets drunk, becomes depressed, and wants his tramp woman back. His wavering state of mind is but another reminder that a fallen sporting hero can never reclaim his once Edenic state. Although Tully returns to train again, we realize that he will never return to his former greatness, for he has been beaten by his most formidable opponent—the system. Concerning Tully's situation, the attitude of Ruben, the manager, is well taken when he laments about his fighters' weaknesses: "They were all so vulnerable, their duration so desperately brief, that all he could do was go on from one to another in quest of that youth who had all that the others lacked" (p. 176). If Ernie Munger is that youth, the evidence in the novel does not emphatically point to it. Even though he wins his fight in another city and feels "he was on his way," his trip back forebodes the advent of another victim of the system. Picked up and cast out in the desert by two lesbians, Ernie Munger rides back home on a bus amid the overbearing imagery of the city, and the novel comes full circle to that point where we first met Billy Tully.

In literature that criticizes the system, it is both interesting and relevant here to note that in recent years a spate of nonfictional accounts have appeared in which sport itself has come under fire as being either too systematized or dehumanizing. Usually written by a former player who has an axe to grind and an opportunity to make a fast dollar, such works, of course, do not come within the purview of this study. However, after reading some of these accounts, one is led to wonder to what extent such material would perhaps qualify as "fiction." A unique work that is worthy of mention here because it appears as the fictional counterpart of the nonfictional exposés is Dan Jenkins's *Semi-Tough* (1972). Even as comic satire this novel incorporates many of the characteristics of the sporting myth discussed here, but the true worth of Jenkins's novel is that it gives the reader a more perceptive picture of the status of organized sport today than many of the so-called nonfictional accounts.

Frustration and alienation continue to dominate the existence of the neo-romantic type of the sporting hero, and in recent fiction we find that in order to cope with the malaise that is his life the neo-romantic retreats into his own private world of fantasy. His sense of mobility urbanized and undermined to the extent that identification with nature is no longer possible, he feels compelled to seek out or create an imaginary world of his own in which he has, at least to the satisfaction of his own mind, some semblance of meaning and identity. In this kind of experience, the microcosm of the retreat is more real and meaningful to the sporting figure than relationship to the actual world.

An outstanding work illustrative of this trend is Robert Coover's *The Universal Baseball Association, Inc.: J. Henry Waugh, Prop.* (1968). The central figure of this brilliant comic novel is an aging accountant who lives not for his work but an imaginary baseball world that he himself has created and peopled with players and officials who, in Henry Waugh's mind, have more identity and significance than his real-life associates. In fact, throughout the novel, the "reality" of his baseball world keeps impinging upon the actual world, causing Henry to daydream and carry on conversations with his "baseball people" even while working or socializing. It is Henry's intimate relationship with his self-created world as opposed to his estranged situation within his day-to-day existence that brings about his encounter experience.

Henry comes off as a sporting character only as he relates to the playing of games, even though his involvement with them has been "all on paper." To Henry's mind, actual physical participation in a game or even watching one is a "bore" because such an experience relates too readily to the world he sees around him. The action of a game, then, is but the outward appearance of the game's true significance, and to Henry the game that translates best into a paper game is baseball, simply because of the infinite possibilities of

> the records, the statistics, the peculiar balances between individual and team, offense and defense, strategy and luck, accident and pattern, power and intelligence. And no other activity in the world had so precise and comprehensive a history, so specific an ethic, and at the same time, strange as it seemed, so much ultimate mystery.[4]

To help capture and dramatize something of the complexity and "ultimate mystery" of the game of baseball, Henry has organized a league comprised of eight teams. In pursuit of the league championship, Henry plays off whole seasons according to an intra-league schedule, with the odds of the teams and the performances of individual players controlled by the roll of three dice. Not

[4]Robert Coover, *The Universal Baseball Association, Inc.* (New York: Random House, 1968), p. 45.

only does the roll of the dice control game performance, but special charts indicate whether a player might injure or even kill himself—rare occurrences, of course, but the Proprietor of the Universal Baseball Association has apparently provided for every possible situation that the game might produce.

When we first meet Henry, he is involved in the playing of season LVI (Henry is 56 years old), and the Haymakers are playing the Pioneers. On the mound for the Pioneers is a youthful ace, Damon Rutherford, who is in the process of pitching a no-hitter, a feat that intrigues Henry not only because of its "unsurpassable perfection" but because it involves his favorite player, with whom Henry equates himself. After Damon pitches his no-hit game to become one of the greatest pitchers in the league's history, Henry's intensity of identification with Damon's achievement is ingeniously expressed by Coover. To celebrate the occasion Henry goes out to his neighborhood tavern, picks up a woman, and brings her back to his apartment. In the ensuing sexual escapade, into which the terminology of baseball is woven in wonderfully comic fasion, Henry Waugh "becomes" Damon Rutherford in action and deed. True to the sporting myth, sexual experience here is intensified through the experience of athletic achievement, even if in this case the accomplishment exists only in the mind.

Going against the usual rotation schedule for a pitcher, Henry, elated over Damon's success, decides to pitch him again the very next night. But unhappily, Damon is struck by a bean ball and killed, an event that unnerves and disenchants Henry but nevertheless one that exemplifies the fatalistic possibilities of the system he has devised: "if a pitcher throws two straight triple ones or sixes and brings on an Extraordinary Occurrence, a third set of ones is a bean ball that kills the batter" (p. 28). Once again the death of a young athlete has brought about an encounter experience for a central character, and Henry feels now that he must either scrap the Association and relate to the real world, or continue to play as he has all along. But with the death of Damon something in Henry has died, and this sense of impending death lends him an even more heightened awareness of the imperfections and absurdities of the world around him—the world of his boss, Horace Zifferblatt, the consummate authority figure, whose cold, businesslike attitude toward life helps Henry to make his decision, even though it costs him his job. "Some people would look on his game, Henry realized, as a kind of running away" (p. 140), but actually he had looked upon his role as an accountant and the day-to-day recording of trifling figures as a "diversion" from what he felt was the more compelling and urgent problems that the roll of the dice created. Thus Henry's unique relationship to the game of baseball has created within him a special kind of mobility sense:

> like a baserunner on the paths, alone in a hostile cosmos, the stars out there in their places, and him trying to dominate the world by stepping on it all. Probably suffered a sense of confinement there in the batter's box, felt the need to strike forth on a meaningful quest of some kind. (p. 141)

Henry's "quest" now is "to play out his part" and finish the season, for "once you set it in motion, you were somehow launched into the same orbit" (p. 142). The idea of the success of a baseball game's being dependent upon the interdependency of its performers is expanded into a metaphor for the interinvolvement of humanity if life is to be a meaningful experience. The fact that Henry's real-life friends do not relate to his game is a comment in itself. He brings Hettie, his tavern companion, home again, but the game mystifies her and she walks out on him. Lou, his well-meaning job associate, attempts to play the game with him, but Lou's indifference toward the game's finer points markedly contrasts with Henry's total involvement in the affairs of his players, both private and on the field. He finishes the season, as he knows he must, but not before he forces the dice to come up with a fatal line drive that kills the player who had beaned his beloved Damon. With this act Henry becomes All-Supreme in his self-created world.

The close of this unique work of fiction, when the activities of Year LVI have evolved to the level of myth and legend, affords Coover a grand opportunity to dramatize Henry Waugh's interrelationship with all the players and officials who ever were a part of the Universal Baseball Association and end the novel on a positive note with the symbolic resurrection of Damon and his comments on the nature of the game and its relationship to life. In its largest sense, *The Universal Baseball Association, Inc.* transcends the resources of the sporting myth in an admirable attempt to crystallize through a game of familiar folk origins the God-Savior-Humanity relationship in our day and time.

Perhaps Frederick Exley has projected the most timely symbol of the neo-romantic's retreat in *A Fan's Notes* (1968) with his anti-hero who identifies with life through the televised exploits of the New York Giants and the performance in particular of one of the team's members, Frank Gifford. The central figure of this novel, an alter ego of the author himself, tells us that

> each weekend I traveled the fifty-odd miles from Glacial Falls to Watertown, where I spent Friday night and all day Saturday in some sustained whisky drinking, tapering off Sundays with a few bottles of beer at The Parrot, eyes fixed

on the television screen, cheering for my team. *Cheering* is a
paltry description. The Giants were my delight, my folly,
my anodyne, my intellectual stimulation.[5]

Like Henry Waugh, Exley is a version of the sporting
hero who does not participate in a physical sense. Having lived in the shadow of a father who was a superior
athlete, Exley identifies with the beauty of the athletic
performance for a special, private reason, as he reveals
to us over the course of his story. Like the sporting hero
of urban background, Exley's life is a failure both mari-
tally and professionally. Needing an escape or retreat,
he relates to his youth and comes up with football as his
great, good place. Actually, Exley's feeling for football
reflects several distinguishing characteristics of the sporting hero. Observe the following confession:

> Why did football bring me so to life? I can't say precisely.
> Part of it was my feeling that football was an island of di-
> rectness in a world of circumspection. In football a man
> was asked to do a difficult and brutal job, and he either did
> it or got out. There was nothing rhetorical or vague about
> it; I chose to believe that it was not unlike the jobs which all
> men, in some sunnier past, had been called upon to do. It
> smacked of something old, something traditional, some-
> thing unclouded by legerdemain and subterfuge. It had
> that kind of power over me, drawing me back with the
> force of something known, scarcely remembered, elusive as
> integrity—perhaps it was no more than the force of a for-
> gotten childhood. Whatever it was, I gave myself up to the
> Giants utterly. The recompense I gained was the feeling of
> being alive. (p. 8)

The need for a feeling of secure status and, of course, a
place to realize this feeling dictate the choice of a "retreat" to view the games, The Parrot bar, which answers
the anti-urban attitude of the myth. To Exley's mind

[5]Frederick Exley, *A Fan's Notes* (New York: Harper & Row, 1968), p. 2.

The Parrot is "ideally isolated on a hill above the city; sitting at the bar I was seldom aware of the city's presence . . . ; sitting at the bar, the city could be thought of as a place remembered, and remembered as if from a great distance" (p. 9). The city is enemy to Exley, and, as we learn, his experiences within it have not been generous in his quest for fame and identity.

His weekend retreats, which grow to be so intense an experience that one Sunday he undergoes what he thinks at the time is a heart attack, and the fear of death, the great antagonist of the sporting figure, afford Exley the opportunity to look back over his life in a series of flashbacks and reveal to the reader the reasons behind his becoming so intense a "fan." Exley's story is really another version of the quest for the American Dream and what happens when one becomes cognizant of the great distance between dream and fact. Having inherited the desire for "wealth and the power that fame would bring" from his fabled father, Exley seeks out his fortune in the great cities of America in the experience-devouring manner of a Thomas Wolfe, but one thing comes back to haunt him—really the basic problem of the sporting figure come to the city—"the inability of a man to impose his dreams, his ego, upon the city" (p. 70). Unable to realize himself, then, Exley carries on his own private war with society, expressing itself essentially as retreat: he spends time in an insane asylum (the ultimate symbol of retreat from society) and he stumbles through a series of jobs and meaningless affairs with women. Finally drink and television football provide him with what he feels are his greatest outlets for status and identity.

Two symbols from Exley's past exist as the keys to comprehending his role as the consummate "fan." He keeps referring to the fact that both Steve Owen, the old coach of the Giants, and Frank Gifford, the star back of the team, have taught him great lessons about life: Owen, "life's hard fact of famelessness," and Gifford, the "realization of life's large promises." Gifford, who had enjoyed great success at New York, symbolizes in Exley's mind the promise of fame, even if he winds up once removed from it as merely a fan:

> I cheered for him with such inordinate enthusiasm, my yearning became so involved with his desire to escape life's bleak anonymity, that after a time he became my alter ego, that part of me that had its being in the competitive world of men; I came, as incredible as it seems to me now, to believe that I was, in some magical way, an actual instrument of his success. Each time I heard the roar of the crowd, it roared in my ears as much for me as him; that roar was not only a promise of my fame, it was its unequivocal assurance. (p. 134)

Fred Exley is a sporting hero who, in his own way, finds the necessary identity and status that such a figure demands. When Gifford endures his career-ending injury, Exley also discovers something about himself that only the more mature kind of sporting hero can face without fear:

> For the first time since the beginning, when so many autumns before we had had the common ground of large hopes, we were, in our separate ways, coming round to the most terrible knowledge of all: we were dying. And that was the inescapable truth. Though I was some time in articulating it, in that limp and broken body against the green turf of the stadium, I had had a glimpse of my own mortality. (p. 359)

Such realization is the beginning of maturity, but Fred Exley, whose destiny has been "to sit in the stands with most men and acclaim others," finds in the long run that his kind of experience has not prepared him to cope with an "incomprehensible America." As the novel ends, Exley responds with the most basic of athletic instincts, but it is really another form of retreat, that of "obsessively *running*."

Another outstanding variation of the retreat from reality as expressed by the neo-romanticists is John Updike's second book in the Rabbit Angstrom saga, *Rabbit Redux* (1971). When we last saw Rabbit he was also "running." In this work we meet him some ten years later, and his pace is somewhat slower than it was in the original novel. Yet he still retains something of the athlete about him: "Though his height, his bulk, and a remnant alertness in the way he moves continue to distinguish him on the street, years have passed since anyone has called him Rabbit."[6] However, one main point about Harry Angstrom is unchanged. He is still at war with his old unfathomable enemy, society. To cope with such an opponent, Harry no longer "runs": instead, he has retreated into the bulwark of conservatism in order to retain and maintain an image of the way he thinks things should be. Unfortunately, the chaotic events of a confused and rapidly moving world keep intruding on his privacy and reminding him that life no longer possesses the precise order of a basketball game, even though Harry still persists in "playing" his own way.

However, nothing appears to be as it once was. His wife, Janice, is now the one running around on him, and with a car salesman whose liberal attitudes about patriotism, Vietnam policy, and the world in general repel Harry and contribute further to the disintegration of his already shaky world. When Janice leaves him to take up with the salesman, Harry retreats even further into his world, symbolized by his mortgaged home in a

[6]John Updike, *Rabbit Redux* (New York: Alfred A. Knopf, 1971), p. 4.

middle-class suburb. Paradoxically, though, he becomes involved with the very forces that would deny him his interpretation of the world as he would like it to be. Jill, a hippie teenager with a drug history, comes to live with him, and in time she makes a revealing analysis of Harry's outlook: "Because of the competitive American context, you've had to convert everything into action too rapidly. Your life has no reflective content; it's all instinct, and when your instincts let you down, you have nothing to trust" (p. 228). Although Harry's athletic days are ostensibly over, characteristics he has acquired from his sporting background have pursued him and still color his attitudes toward life.

Skeeter, a revolutionary black and a friend of Jill's, moves in, precipitating a three-way debate and affording Updike an excellent opportunity to dramatize and comment on many of the serious problems that have polarized contemporary American society. Harry, of course, has a conservative viewpoint toward the black man's plight, yet he still retains something of the sporting hero's admiration for primitiveness:

> The bus has too many Negroes. Rabbit notices them more and more. They've been here all along, as a tiny kid he remembers streets in Brewer you held your breath walking through, though they never hurt you, just looked; but now they're noisier. Instead of bald-looking heads they're bushy. That's O.K., it's more Nature, Nature is what we're running out of. (p. 12)

But even the Negro no longer fits into the world he formerly knew, and the presence of Skeeter in his divided household vividly brings this fact home to him. Skeeter declaims at one point: "We fascinate you, white man. We are in your dreams. We are technology's nightmare." Jill is perhaps closer to the truth of Harry's ambivalent attitude toward the black man when she tells him:

> the reason Skeeter annoys and frightens you is he's opaque, you don't know a thing about his history, I don't mean his personal history so much as the history of his race, how he got here. Things that threaten you like riots and welfare have jumped into the newspapers out of nowhere for you. (p. 229)

Harry's instinctive feeling that problems are resolved in the way one naturally responds to them underscores the major thesis of the novel, that the world will never be the same again and that clinging to old values and standards cannot help resolve the varied problems that continue to crop up every day in an increasingly complex society. Even the metaphor of the game reinforces this contention when Harry attends a baseball game and observes that "something has gone wrong":

> Though basketball was his sport, Rabbit remembers the grandeur of all that grass. . . . There was a beauty here bigger than the hurtling beauty of basketball, a beauty refined from country pastures, a game of solitariness, of waiting, waiting for the pitcher to complete his gaze toward first base and throw his lighning, a game whose very taste, of spit and dust and grass and sweat and leather and sun, was America. . . . Rabbit waits for this beauty to rise in him, through the cheers and the rhythm of innings, the traditional national magic, tasting of his youth; but something is wrong. (p. 83)

Also the game of basketball, which defined Harry's own special kind of mobility, is "different now, everything the jump shot, big looping hungry blacks lifting and floating there a second while a pink palm long as your forearm launched the ball." As if to emphasize even further the change in attitude toward traditional sporting endeavors, Nelson, his thirteen-year-old son, tells him that "sports are square now. Nobody does it" (p. 18).

Perhaps the major symbol of the disintegration of society as Harry has known it is the quality of home life itself, particularly that of his parents, in which the roles of a passive father, an apparently dying mother, and a call-girl type of sister serve to enhance the reality of his own alienated and disordered life. The burning of Harry's home in the suburb and Jill's death in the conflagration, obviously perpetrated by an angered neighborhood incited by tales of sexual perversions, drug addiction, and the presence of a black among them, exist as the final comment on Harry Angstrom's divorce from, and incapacity to contend with, society. It is both ironic and pertinent to this discussion that the foreground action of *Rabbit Redux* is played out against the background of the first landing on the moon in 1969. In stark contrast to the pioneers of the American frontier, the astronauts as space-age pioneers discover only a cold, dead world awaiting them, the antithesis of Natty Bumppo's lush, green territory. The resources of the sporting myth again provide the writer with a telling statement on the predicament of the neo-romantic hero's relationship with modern society.

Is there a concept of the "frontier" still available to the writer of fiction, wherein he can relate the sporting hero to a meaningful pattern of existence? A writer like James Jones seems to think so in his overlong novel, *Go to the Widow-Maker* (1967), when his playwright hero, Ron Grant, points out that "this skindiving stuff . . . is the last frontier left to an individual to do individual work by himself and all on his own as an individual."[7] Feeling

[7]James Jones, *Go to the Widow-Maker* (New York: Delacorte Press, 1967), p. 75.

that his life has become too bureaucratized and dominated by his mistress, Grant escapes to the Caribbean to seek out a "reality of manhood" by learning how to skindive from Al Bonham, a character who comes off in the representative tradition of the sporting hero.

Bonham's life has been an attempt to escape the fetters of civilization, stay uncomplicated, and flee the bondage of women, whom he identifies with merely as sexual objects. When the beautiful Lucky Vivendi comes into Grant's life, things become complicated for him, as does also his relationship with Bonham. Lucky, as an urban sophisticate and enemy of the sporting experience, forces the encounter crisis of the novel with her feminine attitude toward the sporting life: "She had always disliked sports. And 'sportsmen'. And kept as far away from them as possible. There was something funny, sick about them, as if they did all these things because they didn't like women" (p. 262). And later, when she feels that her marriage to Grant is on the rocks:

> all this contemptuousness toward women, all this standing together in a block against the suffocating inroads of womenkind, this *need* to have a world apart that women could not enter, were incapable of understanding, all this had to come from a deep-seated dislike of women, a misogyny, that could only be the result of insecurity and lack of confidence. (p. 371)

Significantly, Ron Grant comes to a reconciliation with Lucky through his realization that the world of Al Bonham is the world of "small boys, playing that they're men." Men, he says, competing with the sexual image of their fathers and knowing they can never achieve it, invent games to be brave and prove their manhood. Despite his discovery of a "new frontier," Ron Grant's awareness of his own social instincts will no longer allow him to participate freely in the world of Al Bonham, who in the true image of the traditional sporting hero must travel his trail alone to adhere to his personal code of being.

As is often the case with literature of an archetypal nature, the critical reputation of works within the scope of the sporting myth in American fiction ranges from those among the finest achievements of literary art to those whose primary appeal is to popular taste. Myth, as the reflection of a culture, it seems, does not confine itself to one level of taste. When a piece of fiction with as high a critical reputation as "The Bear" reflects characteristics in the experience of its hero that are similar to the central figure of "The Eighty-Yard Run," it becomes obvious that what sets one story apart from the other in a critical sense is the degree of intensity and complexity of the author's vision, or in another sense, his craftsmanship in using the resources of the sporting myth. We are aware, too, that the real distinction between the growth in self-knowledge of an Ike McCaslin and the lack of it in a Christian Darling is directly related to the difference in the quality of experience of the hero.

The basically innocent nature of the traditional sporting hero in American fiction delineates a personality made up of deceptively simple characteristics. Closer examination, however, reveals an unusually complicated character, one that in striving for a lost world of innocence paradoxically forces upon himself a complex fate that asserts in most cases a deep sense of alienation. The complexity of the sporting hero in contemporary literature is enhanced, too, by the fact that he is a composite of so many of the characteristics that distinguish the hero of modern fiction. From an existential point of view, mobility, or that quality which defines meaning in motion or action, whether it be expressed as the pursuit of a goal or primarily as flight, emphasizes the sporting hero's intense desire for freedom of personal expression. This desire, of course, springs from his search for identity and the futile attempt to recover his lost Edenic state. On such an insecure quest the hero, particularly if he is of urban background, senses that there are threats to his well-being on all sides: authority, societal ties, and ultimately death, the end of all self-expression.

Such an attitude, we find, has its origin in the mythic experience of Natty Bumppo, who paradoxically lived a life of both flight and advancement toward a goal, thus making him the prototype of the sporting hero in contemporary American literature. The intense worship of self that we find so evident in the experience of our modern-day hero is but the inversion of Natty Bumppo's religion of nature, through which self-definition is realized by identifying with the simple and primitive. Denied such meaningful expression in an increasingly urbanized existence, a Rabbit Angstrom or a Fred Exley can only long for a more meaningful life, and either live in the idealized world of the game or retreat from the actual world. As a result, the most prominent personal defect in the makeup of such characters is their immaturity. Even so, we sense that this deficiency is really the result of the sporting hero's inherent desire to recover the glories of his lost innocence and somehow identify with his environment. If his effort to discover meaning appears at times to be nothing more than the vain and arrogant groping of a frustrated picaro, then we must admire in him at least the validity and intensity of his search for some sense of personal integrity.

In American experience the motivation of the Dream

has been a significant and challenging quest, but today's societal problems have uncovered moral issues that call into question the very meaning and relevance of the Dream itself. Like many of the sporting heroes examined in this book, we have perhaps forgotten what it means to endure, sacrifice, and suffer for those things that make life worthwhile. On the other hand, there is a great deal to be learned from the experience of the sporting hero whose "essential encounter" is determined by the quality of his pursuit and not necessarily by the achievement of a goal. Even in a society that places so much value on material success, such a response can teach us that failure itself can, in a sense, be a kind of success.

Selected Bibliography

Primary Sources

Algren, Nelson. *Never Come Morning.* New York: Harper & Row Perennial Library, 1965.

Bellow, Saul. *Dangling Man.* New York: New American Library Signet Books, 1965.

Cooper, James Fenimore. *The Deerslayer.* New York: Heritage Press, 1961.

Coover, Robert. *The Universal Baseball Association, Inc.: J. Henry Waugh, Prop.* New York: Random House, 1968.

Cheever, John. "O Youth and Beauty!" from *The Housebreaker of Shady Hill.* New York: Harper & Bros., 1958.

Exley, Frederick. *A Fan's Notes.* New York: Harper & Row, 1968.

Faulkner, William. "The Bear" from *Go Down, Moses.* New York: Modern Library, 1942.

Fitzgerald, F. Scott. *The Great Gatsby.* New York: Charles Scribner's Sons, 1953.

Gardner, Leonard. *Fat City.* New York: Dell Books, 1972.

Gordon, Caroline. *Aleck Maury, Sportsman.* New York: Charles Scribner's Sons, 1934.

———. "Old Red" in *Modern Short Stories.* Edited by Arthur Mizener. New York: W. W. Norton & Co., 1962.

Harris, Mark. *Bang the Drum Slowly.* New York: Doubleday Anchor Books, 1962.

Hemingway, Ernest. *Islands in the Stream.* New York: Charles Scribner's Sons, 1970.

————. *The Old Man and the Sea.* New York: Scribner Library, 1952.

————. *The Short Stories of Ernest Hemingway.* Charles Scribner's Sons, 1953.

————. *The Sun Also Rises.* New York: Charles Scribner's Sons, 1926.

Irving, Washington. "The Legend of Sleepy Hollow," from *The Sketch Book.* Dodd, Mead & Co., 1954.

Jenkins, Dan. *Semi-Tough.* New York: Atheneum, 1972.

Johnson, Owen. *Stover at Yale.* New York: Frederick A. Stokes Co., 1912.

Jones, James. *From Here to Eternity.* New York: New American Library Signet Books, 1964.

————. *Go to the Widow-Maker.* New York: Delacorte Press, 1967.

Knowles, John. *A Separate Peace.* New York: Bantam Books, 1966.

Lardner, Ring. *How to Write Short Stories.* New York: Charles Scribner's Sons, 1924.

————. *You Know Me Al.* New York: Charles Scribner's Sons, 1960.

Larner, Jeremy. *Drive, He Said.* New York: Bantam Books, 1971.

Lewis, Sinclair. *Babbitt.* New York: Harcourt, Brace & World, 1922.

London, Jack. "A Piece of Steak," from *Jack London's Tales of Adventure.* Edited by Irving Shepard. Garden City: Hanover House, 1956.

Malamud, Bernard. *The Natural.* New York: Dell Books, 1965.

Marquand, J. P. *H. M. Pulham, Esquire.* Boston: Little, Brown & Co., 1941.

Miller, Perry, ed. *Major Writers of America.* 2 vols. New York: Harcourt, Brace & World, 1962.

Morris, Wright. *The Huge Season.* New York: Viking Press, 1954.

Nemerov, Howard. *The Homecoming Game.* New York: Simon and Schuster, 1957.

Neugeboren, Jay. *Big Man.* Boston: Houghton, Mifflin Co., 1966.

Powers, J. F. *Morte D'Urban.* New York: Doubleday & Co., 1962.

Roth, Philip. *Goodbye Columbus.* New York: Bantam Books, 1963.
Schulberg, Budd. *The Harder They Fall.* New York: Random House, 1947.
Shaw, Irwin. "The Eighty-Yard Run" and "Mixed Doubles," from *Selected Short Stories of Irwin Shaw.* New York: Modern Library, 1961.
Updike, John. "Ace in the Hole," from *The Same Door.* New York: Alfred A. Knopf, 1959.
————. *Rabbit Redux.* New York: Alfred A. Knopf, 1971.
————. *Rabbit, Run.* New York: Crest Books, 1962.
Wallop, Douglas. *So This Is What Happened to Charlie Moe.* New York: W. W. Norton & Co., 1965.
Wolfe, Thomas. "Nebraska Crane," from *You Can't Go Home Again* in *The Thomas Wolfe Reader.* Edited by C. Hugh Holman. New York: Charles Scribner's Sons, 1962.

Secondary Sources

Baumbach, Jonathan. *The Landscape of Nightmare: Studies in the Contemporary American Novel.* New York: New York University Press, 1965.
Beck, Warren. *Man in Motion: Faulkner's Trilogy.* Madison: University of Wisconsin Press, 1961.
Benson, Jackson J. *Hemingway: The Writer's Art of Self-Defense.* Minneapolis: University of Minnesota Press, 1969.
Betts, John R. "The Technological Revolution and the Rise of Sport," *Mississippi Valley Historical Review* 40 (September 1953): 231-56.
Bewley, Marius. *The Eccentric Design: Form in the Classic American Novel.* London: Chatto & Windus, 1959.
Boyle, Robert H. *Sport–Mirror of American Life.* Boston: Little, Brown & Co., 1963.
Brenner, Gerry, "John Updike's Criticism of the 'Return to Nature,'" *Twentieth Century Literature* 12 (April 1966):
Brooks, Van Wyck. *America's Coming-of-Age.* New York: E. P. Dutton & Co., 1958.
Chase, Richard. *The American Novel and Its Tradition.* Garden City: Doubleday & Co., 1957.

Colvert, James B. "Ernest Hemingway's Morality in Action," *American Literature* 27 (November 1955): 372-85.

Cozens, F. W., and Stumpf, F. S. *Sports in American Life.* Chicago: University of Chicago Press, 1953.

Denney, Reuel. *The Astonished Muse.* Chicago: University of Chicago Press, 1957.

Eisinger, Chester E. *Fiction of the Forties.* Chicago: University of Chicago Press, 1963.

Elder, Donald. *Ring Lardner A Biography.* Garden City: Doubleday & Co., 1956.

Fiedler, Leslie. *Love and Death in the American Novel.* New York: Stein & Day, 1966.

Geismar, Maxwell. *American Moderns: From Rebellion to Conformity.* New York: Hill and Wang, 1958.

Gross, John J. *John P. Marquand.* New York: Twayne, 1963.

Gross, Theodore L. *The Heroic Ideal in American Literature.* New York: The Free Press, 1971.

Gwynn, Frederick L., and Blotner, Joseph L., eds. *Faulkner in the University.* Charlottesville: University of Virginia Press, 1959.

Hassan, Ihab. *Radical Innocence: Studies in the Contemporary American Novel.* Princeton, N. J.: Princeton University Press, 1961.

Hoffman, Daniel G. *Form and Fable in American Fiction.* New York: Oxford University Press, 1961.

Hoffman, Frederick J. "Caroline Gordon: The Special Yield," *Critique* 1 (Winter 1956): 29-35.

Howe, Irving. *William Faulkner: A Critical Study.* New York: Vintage Books, 1952.

Kazin, Alfred. *Contemporaries.* Boston: Atlantic-Little, Brown & Co., 1962.

Klein, Marcus. *After Alienation: American Novels in Mid-Century.* Cleveland: The World Publishing Co., 1962.

Lawrence, D. H. *Studies in Classic American Literature.* New York: Boni, 1930.

Lewis, R. W. B. "The Hero in the New World: William Faulkner's 'The Bear'" in *Bear, Man, and God.* Edited by Utley, Bloom, and Kinney. New York: Random House, 1964.

Lynn, Kenneth. *The Dream of Success: A Study of the Modern American Imagination.* Boston: Little, Brown & Co., 1955.

Mizener, Arthur. *The Sense of Life in the Modern Novel.* Boston: Houghton Mifflin Co., 1964.

Morris, Wright. *The Territory Ahead: Critical Interpretations in American Literature.* New York : Atheneum, 1963.

Patrick, Walton R. *Ring Lardner.* New York: Twayne, 1963.

Ringe, Donald. *James Fenimore Cooper.* New York: Twayne, 1962.

Rovit, Earl. *Ernest Hemingway.* New York: Twayne, 1963.

Swados, Harvey. *A Radical's America.* Boston: Little, Brown & Co., 1962.

Taylor, Larry E. *Pastoral and Anti-Pastoral Patterns in John Updike's Fiction.* Carbondale: Southern Illinois University Press, 1971.

Tebbel, John. *From Rags to Riches: Horatio Alger, Jr. and the American Dream.* New York: The Macmillan Co., 1963.

Tunis, John R. *The American Way in Sport.* New York: Duell, Sloan & Pearce, 1958.

Umphlett, Wiley L. "Theme and Structure in John Updike's *Rabbit, Run*," *Laurel Review* 5 (Fall 1965): 35-40.

Utley, Francis Lee; Bloom, Lynn Z.; and Kinney, Arthur F., eds. *Bear, Man, and God: Seven Approaches to William Faulkner's "The Bear".* New York: Random House, 1964.

Weinberg, Helen. *The New Novel in America: the Kafkan Mode in Contemporary Fiction.* Ithaca: Cornell University Press, 1970.

Wilson, Edmund. "The Sportsman's Tragedy," in *The Shores of Light.* New York: Farrar, Straus, and Cudahy, 1952.

Woolf, Virginia. "American Fiction," in *The Moment and Other Essays.* New York: Harcourt, Brace & Co., 1948.

Index

Aaron, Hank, 40
"Action as Form," aesthetic theory of: and Cooper, 44; and Hemingway, 45; and updike, 45
Action: quality of, 21, 25, 194; and Algren, 108; and Cooper, 44; and Faulkner, 61; and Hemingway, 72, 77, 78-80; and Updike, 148, 150
Adams, Richard P., 61n
Alger, Horatio, 36
Algren, Nelson: *Never Come Morning*, 23, 88, 102-9, 114
American Dream, 21, 194-95; and Algren, 109; and Exley, 186; and London, 101; and Malamud, 130, 161, 165, 168
Anderson, Sherwood, 94
Anti-feminine attitude, 26, 29; in Algren, 106-8; in Cooper, 48; in Faulkner, 68; in Gardner, 178; in Harris, 143; in Hemingway, 74-76, 85; in Jones, 112-13, 192; in Lardner, 98-99; in Malamud, 163-64; in Shaw, 125-26
Anti-institutionalism (authoritarianism), 29, 194; and Algren, 105; and Cooper, 183; and Hemingway, 83; and Jones, 110, 112; and Knowles, 135; and

Lardner, 173, 174-75; and Malamud, 161, 166-67; and Updike, 153-54
Anti-society attitude, 88, 112, 188. *See also* Anti-urban attitude
Anti-urban attitude, 10, 23, 88; in Algren, 103, 104-5; in Exley, 185-86; in Faulkner, 65-66; in Gardner, 176-77; in Lardner, 92-97, 100; in Larner, 175-76
Archetypal sources, 20-25, 28-29, 48, 87, 194
Athletic metaphor, *See* Game, metaphor of
Authoritarianism. *See* Anti-institutionalism

Babbit, 36
Ball Four, 90
Baseball, literary use of: in Algren, 108; in Coover, 181; in Harris, 27, 141, 142, 144; in Hemingway, 79-80; in Lardner, 89-90, 97-98; in Malamud, 157-58; in Updike, 190
Basketball, literary use of, 20, 170-71; in Lardner, 173-76; in Neugeboren, 171-73; in Roth, 119-21; in Updike, 149, 150, 151, 188, 190

Beck, Warren, 60
Bellow, Saul, 26, 27
Bench, Johnny, 90
Benson, Jackson J., 22
Bewley, Marius, 44
Book of Sports (James I), 31
Boone, Daniel, 33
Bouton, Jim, 90
Boxing, literary use of, 100-101, 176; in Algren, 102, 103, 108-9; in Gardner, 176-77, 179; in Jones, 27, 102, 110-11; in London, 101-2.
Boyle, Robert H., 22
Bradford, William, 31
Brooks, Van Wyck, 116
Bunyan, Paul, 32
"Busher" attitude, 92-93, 97, 98
Businessman and athletics, 35-36, 116-17

Chase, Richard, 19, 21
Cheever, John: "O Youth and Beauty!", 130, 145, 146-47
Confinement, imagery of: in Algren, 103, 105-6; in Jones, 114-15
Cooper, James Fenimore, 20, 28-29, 39, 43, 47, 55; The Deerslayer, 44, 55; The Prairie, 56
Coover, Robert: The Universal Baseball Association, Inc., 158, 180-84

"Death of Innocence," theme of, 130-45, 134, 137-38, 164
Denney, Reuel, 20
DiMaggio, Joe, 79-80
"Dying-Athlete" theme, 27, 129; in Harris, 131, 141; in Knowles, 131, 134

Elder, Donald, 89, 97
Emerson, Ralph Waldo: "Self-Reliance," 36-37
"Encounter" experience ("Essential Encounter"), 21, 22, 28, 47, 117, 169, 195; in Coover, 183; in Faulkner, 58-61, 69; in Gordon, 49-50, 55, 57; in Harris, 145; in Hemingway, 70-71, 86; in Jones, 192; in Knowles, 131, 138; in Larner, 175; in Malamud, 157, 162
Existentialism, 25
Exley, Frederick: A Fan's Notes, 184-88

"Failure of Love," theme of, 26, 130
"Failure of Vision" as metaphor, 109, 117
Faulkner, William, 45, 55, 70, 78; "The Bear," 18, 24, 47, 58-69, 193
Fear of death, expression of, 194; in Cooper, 55-56; in Cheever, 146-47; in Exley, 187; in Gordon, 55-56; in Larner, 174; in Updike, 155-56.
Fiedler, Leslie, 26
Fishing, literary use of, 48; in Gordon, 47, 51, 53; in Hemingway, 72-73, 76-77, 81
Fitzgerald, F. Scott, 117
Folk hero and sporting hero, 32-33, 90
Football, literary use of, 116; in Exley, 184-85; in Fitzgerald, 117; in Marquand, 117-18; in Nemerov, 118
Franklin, Benjamin, 34-36
"Frontier sense," 23, 34, 46, 191
Frye, Northrop, 129

Game, metaphor of, 20, 22, 23; in Hemingway, 17-18, 70-71; in Knowles, 132; in Lardner, 94; in Updike, 150-51, 156, 190
Gardner, Leonard: Fat City, 101, 176-79
Gifford, Frank, 184, 187
Golf, literary use of, 36
Gordon, Caroline, 60; Aleck Maury,

Sportsman, 47, 49-57; "Old Red," 49, 52, 53, 56
The Great Gatsby, 117
"Great, good place," image of, 129; in Cooper, 43; in Exley, 185; in Harris, 140; in Hemingway, 72, 74; in Knowles, 132; in Neugeboren, 172
The Greening of America, 34

The Harder They Fall, 101
Harris, Mark: *Bang the Drum Slowly*, 27-28, 129, 131, 139-45
Hassan, Ihab, 70, 160
Hegel, 137
Hemingway, Ernest, 17-18, 22, 45, 55, 68, 70-71, 119, 177; "Big Two-Hearted River," 42, 72-73; "The Doctor and the Doctor's Wife," 74; "The End of Something," 74; "Fathers and Sons," 76; "Fifty Grand," 101; "Indian Camp," 74; *Islands in the Stream*, 18, 72, 76-77, 81; *The Old Man and the Sea*, 48, 70, 72, 77-86; "The Short and Happy Life of Francis Macomber," 71; "Soldier's Home," 75; "The Three Day Blow," 74-75; *The Sun Also Rises*, 72; "The Undefeated," 76
Howe, Irving, 39
Hunt, metaphor of, 43, 59; in Algren, 104; in Faulkner, 58-59, 62
Hunting, literary use of, 48; in Algren, 104; in Cooper, 43; in Faulkner, 58-59, 62, 63, 70; in Gordon, 47, 56; in Hemingway, 71

Idealism (Emersonian), 28, 36-37
Illusion vs. reality, theme of, 137-39
Immortality, quest for, 23, 62-63, 74, 131
Individualism, expression of: in Harris, 141, 144-45; in Jones, 27, 110, 114-16; in Larner, 176;

through "Dying Athlete," 131
Innocence vs. experience, theme of, 24; in Knowles, 134-35, 136; in Malamud, 158-60, 162. *See also* Illusion vs. reality
Irony (ironic mode), use of, 20, 35, 42, 95, 129, 130, 142
Irving Washington, 29, 87; "The Legend of Sleepy Hollow," 39-43

Jenkins, Dan, 180
Jung, Carl, 21
Johnson, Owen, 38
Jones, James: *From Here to Eternity*, 27, 88, 102, 110-16, 176; *Go to the Widow-Maker*, 191-93

Kazin, Alfred, 119
Klein, Marcus, 160
Knowles, John: *A Separate Peace*, 38, 129, 131-39

Lardner, Ring, 19, 41, 88, 89; "Alibi Ike," 96-97; "Champion," 101; "Horsehoes," 42; *You Know Me Al*, 87, 90-100
Larner, Jeremy: *Drive, He Said*, 173-76
Lawrence, D. H., 23
Lewis, Sinclair, 35, 116
London, Jack, 101, 109; "A Piece of Steak," 101-2
Lynn, Kenneth, 101

Malamud, Bernard: *The Natural*, 18, 24, 40, 130, 156-68, 171, 173
Marquand, J. P., 35; *H. M. Pulham, Esq.*, 117
Melville, Herman, 175
Merriwell, Frank, 37, 44, 90
Mizener, Arthur, 71
Mobility, significance of, 28, 31, 32, 39, 45, 130, 169, 171, 172, 180, 194; in Cheever, 147; in Coover, 183; in Faulkner, 60-61; in Gordon, 52, 53, 57, 60; in Jones,

111-12; in Malamud, 161-63; in Updike, 148
Morris, Wright, 57; *The Huge Season,* 17, 56
Morton, Thomas, 31-32

Narcissism, 33-34, 91, 146
Naturalism, 88, 103
Nature: as necessary environment, 48; interdependence of, 80-82; society as enemy of, 22-23, 87
Nemerov, Howard: *The Homecoming Game,* 118
Neo-romanticism, 20, 29; 128-68; heroic type defined, 128-30; recent trends, 180-91
Neugeboren, Jay: *Big Man,* 171-73

O'Hara, John, 35, 116
"Outsider," image of, 38, 39-40, 87; in Algren, 108; in Irving, 41-42; in Lardner, 41-42
Owen, Steve, 186, 187

Playing field as symbol of "Forest-Frontier," 38, 43, 142
Podhoretz, Norman, 160n
Powers, J. F: *Morte D'Urban,* 36
Primitive virtues, worship of: in Faulkner, 66-67; in Gordon, 53-54; in Knowles, 137; in Updike, 149, 154-55
Puritanism, 31-35
"Pursuit" concept, 48-49, 130; in Cheever, 147; in Faulkner, 60; in Gordon, 50, 51, 57; in Knowles, 133; in Malamud, 157, 168

"Retreat" concept, 42-43; in Hemingway, 72, 73; in Jones, 112
Romantic tradition (Cooper), 43-46
Roth, Philip: *Goodbye, Columbus,* 88, 119-23
"Rules" of forest or wilderness, 43, 45, 59, 63, 67

Satire, use of: in Irving, 39-43; in Nemerov, 118; in Roth, 88, 122; in Shaw, 88
Schulberg, Budd, 101
"Search for maturity," theme of, 88, 116-27
"Search for self," theme of, 27, 122-23; in Updike, 145-56
Self-determination (Hemingway), 84-85, 85-86
Semi-Tough, 180
Shaw, Irwin: "The Eighty-Yard Run," 25, 88, 123-27, 128, 193; "Mixed Doubles," 150-51
Skindiving, literary use of, 191-92
Slatoff, Walter J., 61n
Sport as system, 118, 179-80
Sporting hero, myth of: as "Innocent," 23, 24; as "Outsider," 29; classic characteristics of, 28-29; fictional pattern of, 21; literary origins, 39; literary traditions of, 27-28; origin of, 31; primal unity, quest for, 64, 69; psychological basis for, 21-22; summary of characteristics, 193-95
"Sportsman's code," 20, 44
Stein, Jean, 61n
Stover at Yale, 38
Success myth ("Success ethic"), 28, 34-35, 37, 101
Suffering, role of: in Hemingway, 82-83; in Malamud, 130, 165, 167, 168
Swados, Harvey, 119

Tennis, literary use of, 150-51
Thoreau, 51, 52, 55
Tunis, John, 22

Updike, John, 18, 24, 25, 145; "Ace in the Hole," 153; *Rabbit Redux,* 153, 188-91; *Rabbit, Run,* 10, 20, 45, 130, 147-56

Walden, 51
Wallop, Douglas, 23
Wilderness, metaphor of: in Algren,
104; in Knowles, 136-37; in
Malamud, 158-59; in Updike,
155-56

Wolfe, Thomas, 162, 186
Woolf, Virginia, 19

You Can't Go Home Again, 162